Meetup Organizer Step-by-Step Success Guide

Road map to success for Meetup Organizers and their Leadership Teams

- What is a Meetup?
- Why you should start a group?
- How to begin?
- What to expect?
- Where should you meet?
- Meetup leaders share success stories and best practices.
- Online Meetup Organizer Groups, how to connect and get involved?

Just finished reading Meetup Organizer Step-by-Step Success Guide. *It's all the info you need to start your own group! It answered all of my questions and it was oh, so easy to read.* –Lee Mirabal, CEO Voicemarketing, Inc., Producer and Co/Host of eBay Radio

When Stephanie decides to do something, she does it right. That's why I was honored when Stephanie asked me to help her organize a social media Meetup several years ago. With all of her experience with the Dallas eBaybes & eMales, she knew just the way to do it. And she was right, we were successful immediately and grew quickly. This book is based on Stephanie's experience with Meetup and her desire to share that experience. Everyone can learn from this very well-written book. Stephanie is very organized and has a knack of explaining things in a way that is easy to understand. That's what makes her a great teacher and now a writer. If you have any desire to start a Meetup on any subject, this is a must-read book. If you follow it, you will be successful. –Sandy Norton

Stephanie Inge is one of the most delightful and honest people I've ever met. She is smart, funny, and a great teacher and mentor for all people wanting to learn. She created one of the largest Meetup groups in the USA and also started a successful social media marketing group in Dallas, Texas. She is a dedicated eBay Education Specialist and teaches eBay classes at the local colleges. She has been invited to speak at eBay social events, as well as at eBay University. This is her first book, so please be prepared to expect more in the future. This book provides step-by-step instructions on how you, too, can start a Meetup Group in your area and share your passion, no matter if it's an Art Appreciation Group or a Cycling Group. I am proud to have known Stephanie all these years and so happy to belong to The Dallas eBaybes & eMales Meetup Group. –Grenda Walton, eBay Specialist

Look up the term 'eBay Meetup' and you should see a picture of Stephanie Inge! Stephanie created the first eBay Meetup, the Dallas eBaybes and

eMales, and it continues to be one of the largest and most successful Meetup Groups in the country. I have personally attended several of Stephanie's Meetups and always come away with more knowledge in addition to having FUN! I'm excited to see Stephanie share her knowledge and experience with others in this book. –Chris Green, Director, ScanPower.com

Bravo! Finally, a powerful step-by-step guide for Meetup organizers in regard to establishing and running a successful Meetup group. I wish I would have had a great tool like this book when I started on Meetup. A must read for anyone interested in joining and running a Meetup Group. –Steve Kuntz, Organizer, DFW Interactive Marketing & Internet

Meetup Organizer Step-By-Step Guide *by top Meetup organizer Stephanie Inge is exactly what potential Meetup organizers and operators need. In this guide, Stephanie instructs the reader in a simple conversational tone while presenting complex material in a superbly organized manner. This is a highly detailed guide that teaches the basics, such as how to charge dues and when and where to meet. Then, she skillfully blends in advanced marketing information on finding speakers, promoting the group, and organizing the format. She integrates the benefits of social media such as Facebook and Twitter to grow both attendance and keep interest alive and dynamic for Meetups.* Meetup Organizer Step-By-Step Guide *makes it fun and easy to start and run a Meetup in your area and you have the benefit of Stephanie's years of experience to walk you through the process.* –Joyce Banbury, eBay Certified Education Specialist; Organizer: Kansas Jubilee Conference; http://auctionbbs.com

In 2010, when I wanted to start up a group of local eBay sellers, I contacted Stephanie as she'd run a successful Meetup group for several years. She told me how to get started, and our group is healthy because of her input! As I reviewed this book, I could see her suggestions making our group even healthier, more interesting and more successful. Whether you want to start an eBay Meetup group or any other group, you'll find some great info within! –Sally Milo, Tucson eBay Sellers Meetup Group

Meetup Organizer Step-by-Step Success Guide *is detailed, helpful, and easy-to-read. Written in a conversational style, you will feel like Stephanie is right there rooting for you to succeed.* –Tony Cecala, DFW WordPress Meetup Organizer

The Meetup Organizer

Step-by-Step Success Guide

Meetup Organizer Step-by-Step Success Guide

Road map to success for Meetup Organizers and their Leadership Teams

Stephanie E. Inge

First Published by SEI Press, October 2013

ISBN-13: 978-0615905488
ISBN-10: 061590548X

Printed in the United States of America

Cover Design: Nikki Bassham

Because of the dynamic nature of the Internet, any web addresses or links contained in this book may have changed since publication and may no longer be valid.

Dedication

To fellow eBay Meetup Organizers throughout the world, past, present and future, I dedicate this book to you and to all the members of The Dallas eBaybes and eMales and the DFW Social Media Marketing Group with special recognition to my long-time, dedicated leadership teams: Terry Thayer, Dan Goins, Paula Barnes, and Lissa Duty.

Special thanks go out to my daughter Brooklyn for her unyielding confidence in me and her constant encouragement to write this book, my dear friend Grenda Walton for her inspiration, Chris Green for his encouragement, Joyce Banbury for lighting the fire, and last, but certainly not least, Jim "Griff" Griffith for writing the Foreword for this book.

Acknowledgments

With the most sincere thanks to:

- Chris Taylor, Bay Area eBay Sellers
- Michelle Gauvreau, Connecticut eBay Sellers
- Bobbi Miller, Seacoast eBay Sellers
- Bruce Zalkin, Sarasota eBay Sellers
- Robbin Levin, New England eBay & Ecommerce Sellers
- Rich Siok, The Chicagoland eBay & eCommerce Sellers
- Danni Ackerman, Las Vegas eBay Amazon Ecommerce Online Sellers
- Jim "Griff" Griffith, Dean of eBay Education and author of *The Official eBay Bible*
- Brooklyn Calloway, Editor
- Liz Partlow, Wordsmith
- Scott Heiferman, CEO/Co-Founder Meetup.com

Contents

Foreword

Selling on eBay can be many things at different times: profitable, exasperating, rewarding, exhausting, fulfilling and a never-ending education in the ins and outs, ups and downs of running your own business. One unavoidable aspect of running your own business on eBay, usually out of your house or basement or garage: we sellers tend to work alone most of the time, with our only silent companions being boxes, packing peanuts, rolls of bubble wrap and shelves of merchandise we have yet to list or have to ship.

Besides being business people, we are all also humans who occasionally need a break from the solitary activities of listing and packing and bookkeeping and the endless quest to keep the customer satisfied and delighted. It's no wonder that so many sellers across the USA are forming ecommerce meet-up groups where sellers can get together, relax over good food and good company to share war stories, tips, and advice and to commiserate, good-naturedly of course, about the recent eBay releases and changes.

As the founder and manager of the longest running eBay sellers group – The Dallas eBaybes and eMales – Stephanie Inge, besides being a paragon of good old Texas hospitality, also knows a thing or two about how to start, manage, and grow an eBay-seller Meetup Group. She'd be the first to tell you, it isn't always easy but in the same breath, she would do whatever it takes to convince you that it's well worth the effort (and she's always been at the ready to offer assistance to anyone interested in starting their own group). And what better way is there for sharing her experience and expertise than through a book!

And so for you who are on the verge of starting an eBay Meetup Group, rest assured: you are in the very best of hands. I can think of no better guide through the process than my friend, Stephanie Inge. Enjoy!

Griff (Jim Griffith)

Welcome To My World

My name is Stephanie Inge. I started selling on eBay in March 1999, became the first-ever college eBay instructor in 2002, received certification as an Education Specialist and was trained by eBay in October 2004, shortly after their training program was introduced. Some of my accomplishments that may be of interest to you:

- member of eBay *Voices of the Community,* January 2006 (#34)
- eBay Powerseller of the Month February 2006
- eBay Instructor of the Month, June 2006
- Texas State Representative for *The United States of eBay* September 2006
- lobbied Congress March 2013, and
- invited by eBay, Inc., to teach advanced classes for *eBay University,* held in Dallas, Texas in 2007.

Growing up, games like house, school, and store were my games of choice, provided I could be the leader, i.e., the mom, teacher, or cashier. I enjoyed keeping people and things organized and moving toward our goals, even then.

Fast forward to 1979, my beautiful daughter, Brooklyn, was born and in 1988 along came my son, Ryder, and for awhile, I was a mom that liked going to garage sales. My passion for that "treasure hunting" had actually begun when I was a teenager and just grew stronger over time.

In 1998 while attending classes at Richland College, I learned about a new website called eBay, and that's when the light bulb came on. At that time, I was also operating an unsuccessful antique booth and knew that eBay was the golden ticket to combine my childhood games with my enthusiasm for treasure hunting. The perfect combination for me to live the American dream. Within a month or two, I had liquidated all of the inventory and was well on my way to becoming a successful eBay entrepreneur. I taught my first private eBay class in September 1999 and became the first-ever college eBay instructor in 2002 for Dallas County Community Colleges.

Warning: working out of a home office in front of a computer day in and day out can be isolating and monotonous. Then, a magazine article about a casual meet-and-greet of eBay sellers in Atlanta ignited a spark, an idea that later became the first ever official eBay sellers' group: *Dallas eBaybes & eMales,* formed in January 2002. Some have even said that I became a true pioneer in this field.

The initial meeting of *Dallas eBaybes & eMales* took place on a cold, gloomy January evening in 2002, three years before Meetup came into existence and "social media" was only a gleam in the founders' eyes. There were sixteen of us at that first meeting, but it lasted a couple of hours and was well received by everyone who attended. Meetings continued at the same location, Chili's Restaurant, for several months, and more people came until we eventually outgrew the small private room.

In the early days, the only forms of communication to market and promote our eBay group were email, discussion forums, newsgroups, and eBay discussion groups. I began to realize that meeting with a peer group was so satisfying that there must be many who are not part of a professional society and feel the need of sharing experiences and knowledge just as we were doing in our eBay group.

It was about then that I discovered Meetup.com and found the path leading to fulfillment of my wish to share our experiences.

From the Meetup.com *About* page:

> ***Meetup is*** *the world's largest network of local groups. Meetup makes it easy for anyone to organize a local group or find one of the thousands already meeting up face-to-face. More than 9,000 groups get together in local communities each day, each one with the goal of improving themselves or their communities.*

Meetup is a website for organizers and leaders of local groups. Now, there are tens of thousands of Meetup groups throughout the world, covering a wide range of topics.

In 2005, we initiated our own Meetup groups here in Dallas. Finding like-minded peers with vested interests in similar topics became a piece of cake compared to the communication processes of the past! Out with the old ways and in with the new.

Many of the original members continue to attend monthly meetings, and because of the greatness that is Meetup and the onslaught of social media tools, membership has grown substantially. There are approximately 350 members at this time in our group. Venues have changed many times, and we have welcomed many influential guest speakers, including the Dean of eBay Education, Jim "Griff" Griffith, Sharon McBride from eBay Government Relations, aka eBay Main Street (http://www.ebaymainstreet.com/), and Jeff Terrell, Director of Community Relations at eBay, Inc.

In March 2009, I was fortunate enough to team up with Sandy Norton, a local "techie" and social media enthusiast, to create the DFW Social Media Marketing Group. This Meetup has experienced explosive growth. It is 1,400 members strong;

our monthly meetings feature guest speakers, as well as the occasional expert panel, on all things related to social media.

In this book, my plan is to present the concept of Meetup groups and lead you, the interested reader, into forming your own Meetup group so that you and others like you can benefit from the camaraderie and shared information that all Meetups so enjoy.

Good reading,
Steph

Disclaimer

Meetup, Inc., has no affiliation with this book and is not responsible for its content. For Meetup recommendations or questions, please visit the official Meetup site (http://www.meetup.com/).

The Meetup name and logo and other related trademarks are the property of Meetup, Inc.

I'm not employed by or compensated by Meetup.com to advertise or promote the website. I have written this guide from the perspective of subscriber, organizer, and huge fan. I speak from first-hand knowledge and experience as an organizer of three Meetup Groups since 2005.

Information contained in this book is based on personal experience, the experience and recommendations of other Meetup Organizers, and a compilation of information obtained from research on the Meetup website, Wikipedia, and other Internet resources.

1 - What is Meetup?

Meetup.com
Meetup helps like-minded people connect with others who share their *interest* or *cause*. People are able to form *local community groups* that meet on a regular basis. Important to note, it is free to join Meetup.com and the only time you'll pay is if you decide to start your own group and become a community leader/organizer.

Meetup believes that the world will be a better place when everyone has access to a people-powered local Meetup Group. Meetup Groups help people:

- find others
- get involved locally
- learn, teach, and share ideas
- make friends and have fun
- rise up, stand up, unite, and make a difference
- be a part of something bigger - both locally and globally

For even more information about Meetup.com, please visit:

- their blog (http://meetupblog.meetup.com/) and
- *About* page (http://www.meetup.com/about/).

In a recent article from *TechCrunch* (http://techcrunch.com/):

> *According to Meetup CEO Scott Heiferman, despite the company's age, it has only been over the past year to eighteen months that he feels Meetup really reached the "tipping point" in terms of network effects. "We're growing faster than ever right now," he says. "We kind of like being a little under the radar – a lot of people use Meetup, but people don't think of us as the 'hot' startup. That's fine by us. We're coming up on 20 million members, and we just hit 3 million people [going to meetups] this past month." (Meetup currently has 14.5 million members and is planning to add 5 million more this year.)*
>
> *At times, the company is hosting as many as 20,000 meetups daily, he tells us. It has 200,000 groups total. In addition, Meetup has been profitable for three years, thanks to its subscription business which charges organizers $15 per month to run their groups, equating to an over $20 million annualized run rate.*

Who Runs the Meetup Groups?

Meetup Groups are run by individuals referred to as Organizers and/or Leaders and are typically helped by Assistant Organizers and/or Co-organizers.

Organizers are required to pay organizer dues to Meetup in order to operate their groups. They can add their Meetup events to their Meetup group calendar and Meetup will keep track of RSVP's and send out automatic email reminders. The organizer will decide for or against a membership policy.

Organizers also manage and approve the members of their Meetup Group. Meetup.com is a valuable tool for organizers and leaders of professional organizations and local groups that meet on a regular basis.

Most Organizers appoint a leadership team that can consist of co-organizers or assistant organizers. For special events, they can also enlist the help of event hosts for additional help.

What Type of Meetup Groups Are Available?
There are literally hundreds, if not thousands, of Meetup groups including, but certainly not limited to, WordPress, toastmasters, singles travel, business networking, Joomla, entrepreneurs, hiking, skiing, adventure, retro computing, insanity, P90X, real estate investors, small business, search engine marketing, public speaking, mommy workouts, social cigar professionals, business investing, wine lovers, Italian speakers, ex-British patriots, event planning, Christian singles, atheists, Hispanic professionals, black professionals, women in business, ukulele players, science fiction lovers, etc.

2 – Why Should You Start a Meetup Group?

The Reasons Are Many

There are so many reasons to start a Meetup group, and if you ask a handful of people, you'd likely get five different reasons. A very important reason that many of us share is the need to connect. Meetup has put the 'social' back into social media!

"None of us are as smart as all of us" epitomizes the heart and soul of Meetup. I learn something new at every Meetup event.

Meetup.com provides organizers with a host website that is customizable and offers a plethora of online tools, which has proven to be a lifesaver. This website has played an integral part in the success of my interest groups. It will make your role as the Meetup organizer as easy as a click of a few buttons. They take care of the "heavy lifting" by automating many of the clerical tasks, such as sending out scheduled reminders, tracking RSVP's, keeping up with your calendar, etc.

3 – Before Starting Your Own Meetup Group

In order to join or start a Meetup group, you must first join Meetup.com and create a Meetup profile. Important to note that there are two types of profiles for Meetup; one is a general profile created when you join the website, and the second is a group profile created when you join an individual group. Group profiles vary, based on the criteria set forth by each group's organizer.

Now that you have the idea of building a Meetup group, it is important to determine if a group like yours already exists. Do preliminary research on the Meetup site using keywords that pertain to your group. If the search does not produce any results, try a few other related keywords. If there are no groups pertaining to your topic, now is the perfect time to start one and become a local community leader.

However, if you find that there is a group similar to yours, find out answers to the following questions:

- Are they active?
- How often do they meet?
- When was their last meeting?
- When was the group started?
- How many members do they have?
- Where do they meet?

Don't be discouraged if there is a similar group. Many large cities and metropolitan areas can support multiple groups on the same topics. If your city is too small for more than one group, join the existing group, get involved, and think about joining their leadership team.

Join a Meetup Group

Find a few Meetup groups that sound interesting. Join, attend a few meetings, and get a feel for what works and what doesn't.

Joining a Meetup group is simple. When you come across one that sounds interesting, just click the *Join us!* link on the right side of the navigation bar. Once you join, you will be required to complete a basic profile and upload a photo or avatar. A group profile is a description of you for the benefit of the other members of the group to help everyone get to know each other. There is no limit to how many groups you are allowed to join.

Meetup groups are either open to everyone or private. The private groups require organizer approval before new members are able to join. If you desire to be a part of a private group, once you submit your profile, you'll see the following message, which indicates that the group organizer has been notified of your pending approval request:

> *Thanks! Your information has been saved and your request for membership has been sent to the Meetup's Organizer. You should hear back shortly.*

Your group profile is a short page about you and is specific to each group that you join. Think of it this way – if you compose a resume for position at a marketing firm, it may look different than the skills that you would highlight for a volunteer position in the nursery at your local church. Different groups call for different introductions.

The membership link can be found in the top right corner of the group's home page or by clicking the *Members* link located on the toolbar. After clicking on the *Members* link, you'll be taken to the *Members* page where you'll see the *View Your Profile* link.

As you get to know the other members of the group and have attended enough meetings that you feel comfortable with the way that group works, dive in head first. Take the plunge into leadership and volunteer to be an assistant organizer. Whoa, now that's a step. Assistant organizers get a first-hand look at the whole picture; you would get a good idea of how to run meetings as well as learning what goes on behind the scenes.

Finally, you'll be ready to start your own Group!

4 – Becoming a Meetup Organizer

Allow me to be the first to congratulate you on the decision to start your own Meetup group. It has been a labor of love and brought so much joy to my life; my hope will be that your experience is just as rewarding.

This Meetup guide will walk you through each step by providing everything you need to know to get started on the right foot. I highly recommend connecting with other organizers by visiting the Meetup forum (http://www.discussmeetup.com/forum/) and Facebook Meetup organizer groups

(https://www.facebook.com/groups/302209236514960/?ref=br_t).

In addition to these resources, you now have your very own Meetup mentor, ME! I'm as close as a keystroke, and I pride myself on timely responses. Do not ever hesitate to contact me with questions.

Start by naming your new Meetup group. Avoid cutesy names, puns, play on words, acronyms, etc., as the title of a Meetup group is crucial to future members' being able to find it. If, for instance, you want to create an eBay Meetup group, include the word *eBay* in the name. That may seem obvious, but many Meetup groups' names are vague and, therefore, difficult to find. By including specific key words, potential members will automatically know what your group is about and, even more importantly, your group will pop up in key word searches. Include other relevant keywords, depending on what topics you intend to cover.

As a Meetup Organizer and community leader, it's important to make good decisions on behalf of your members and always consider the interest of the group first. Without members, there would be no group and as they say, "There is no I in team or group." Be decisive, stay focused on topics of interest, plan ahead, and keep things simple and stress-free.

Not ready to take on the task and/or responsibility all by yourself? No problem! You may already have a network of peers and acquaintances who would be interested in joining or becoming co-organizer. Make a list of possible candidates and send them an email or give them a call to see if they'd be interested in a joint venture as Meetup organizers.

Organizer Dues

Meetup organizers are required to pay monthly dues (currently $19.00) for up to three groups. To update, manage, or cancel your organizer dues, click the *Organizer Dues* option under *Account* in the top right corner.

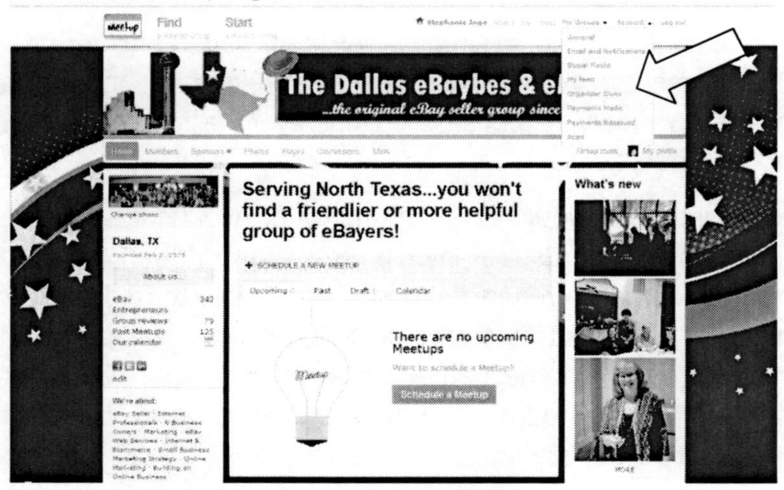

On the *Organizer Dues* page, you'll be able to perform any of the following tasks:

- View your current plan
- Find out your organizer dues renewal date
- See full payment history

- Change your organizer dues' plan
- Update credit card information
- Cancel your renewal
- Restart lapsed or canceled organizer dues

How to Change to a Different Organizer Dues Plan

From the *Organizer Dues* page click the link that says *change* next to your current organizer dues rate.

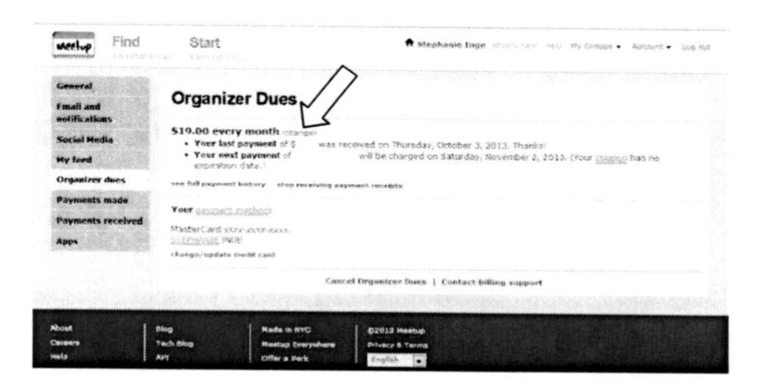

On the following page, choose the new plan, and click *Change*.

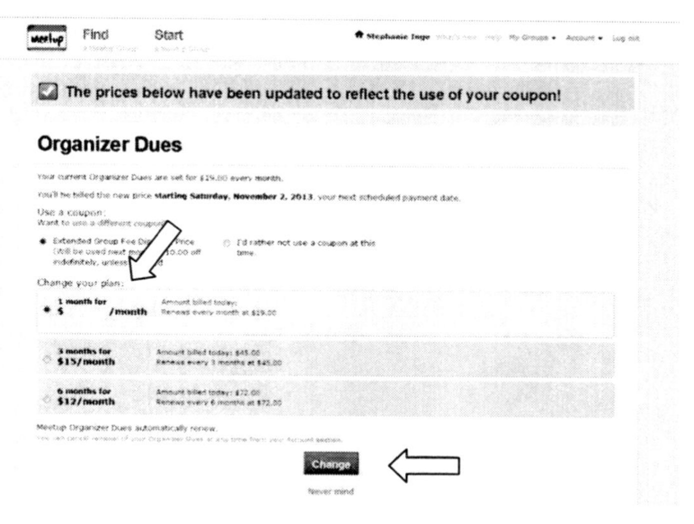

The new plan and rate will go into effect on the date your organizer dues are set to renew.

5 – Getting Started With Your New Meetup Group

First Things First!

This Meetup Guide was created for people just like us who sometimes need a little guidance getting started. Until you gain the confidence to sprout your wings and fly solo, this guide will be a valuable resource to help you organize and plan your new Meetup group.

Organizing your very own Meetup group can be a lot of fun, but at times it can also be challenging. Remember that you are the Organizer/Founder, and since you're in charge, keep it stress-free.

Once you've come up with a name for your new group and registered it with Meetup.com, there are a few more things to do before planning your first event.

- Create a free, dedicated email address for your group. I recommend Gmail for several reasons; however, any web-based email provider will work. Separate email accounts will help to keep Meetup messages organized and separate from your personal email.
- Meetup provides organizers with a built-in email messaging system to communicate with members, but they do not share member email addresses with organizers.
- There are a few options for sending email messages within the Meetup message system, and individual messages can even be sent between members, unless the member has blocked their email.

Choose Up To Fifteen Topics

Organizers can list their Groups under fifteen separate topics related to the group. Topics help determine who will be notified when your new group is announced. Topics also help people find and locate your group on the site when searching particular topics. Topics attached to your group help the Meetup search engines optimize group searches conducted by members wanting to find particular groups.

For example, let's say you're starting an eBay Seller Group. eBay would be your first obvious pick for a topic, but you would want to list your Meetup group under the e-commerce and small business topics as well.

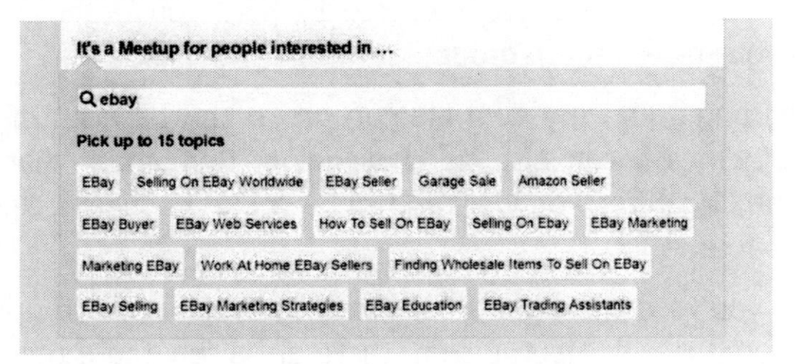

Once you've selected all of the relevant and appropriate topics, Meetup will provide a list of people in your area who are interested in these topics. Better yet, Meetup will automatically send them an email to invite them to join your group! How cool is that?

Setting Profile Requirements for Your Meetup Group

Organizers can require members to create a group profile prior to joining the Meetup group. This profile is limited to your group's use and not to be confused with the Meetup.com profile.

To do this, go into *Group Settings* from your *Group Tools.* Then click on *Your Members.* Scroll down to the *New Member Profile Requirements* bullet.

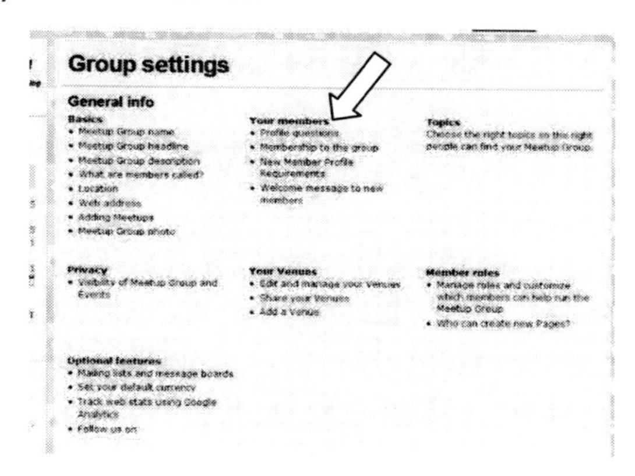

Introduction asks members "Why did you want to join this group?"

Photo: The member must upload a profile photo before they can join your Meetup group.

Profile questions: These are the questions in a member's profile that you create. Potential members must fill out all of your profile questions. You will need to select this option in order to add profile questions.

If you also set your membership to *approval only* (private), you can ensure that members have completed their profile and have provided appropriate answers and/or profile photo.

Sample Profile Questions

- What is your eBay user ID?
- How did you come up with your eBay user ID?

- How did you hear about us?
- How long have you been selling on eBay?
- Do you sell on any other websites? If so, which ones?
- What is your current Feedback score and rating?
- What do you hope to gain by being a member of this eBay seller's Meetup group?
- What topics would you like to discuss in future Meetups?
- What type of items do you sell?
- Would you be willing to teach a class at an upcoming Meetup? If so, what would the topic be?

Writing Your Meetup Group Description

It's time to write. Don't worry if you have writer's block or are feeling overwhelmed. You're completely normal and definitely not the only one. Think of it this way: it's not a novel, just a short description, and it can be tweaked as often as necessary. The important thing is to get something posted on your Meetup site so that people can find you.

Try browsing the Meetup site for similar topics and groups. Read their descriptions. Before you know it, you'll be coming up with your own ideas. Get those creative juices flowing and remember to be friendly, upbeat, clear, and to the point. Your group description is how others will decide if your Meetup group is a good fit and if they'd like to join.

When writing your description, remember the "5W's and the H": who, what, when, where, why, and how. Answering these simple questions will greatly help you to explain what your group is about. They will guide you in your writing by helping you explain who should join, why they should join, and what they can expect. It is important to establish your expectations of them as well. As learned in previous chapters, remember to use relevant keywords in your description. Relevant keywords help new members to find you.

How to Use the Event Description Editor

Each Meetup description should contain a detailed description of what to expect at the event. This will help your members decide if the event is one they should attend. Feel free to add photographs, links to resources, and basic formatting options to emphasize important information. Due to a recent revision, it easy for Organizers to create Meetup events that have a consistent look and feel across all platforms. (See more detail below in section on describing your first event.)

Add a Video to your Meetup Description

Adding a video to your Meetup group description or one of your group pages can really help to create a buzz. Videos get your Members excited about the group and its activities.

These are the video platforms that are currently supported by Meetup: YouTube, Google Video, Vimeo, Flickr, Ustream and Livestream. Videos must be between 200 pixels and 470 pixels wide.

To start, head over to the *Basics* page in *Group Settings* under *Group Tools*. You'll want to scroll down to the Group description section.

Hit the *HTML* button in the tool bar above your Meetup group description. A small window will pop up. Once you see the pop-up menu, place your cursor wherever you'd like to insert the video, and paste in the HTML embed code. Click *Update*.

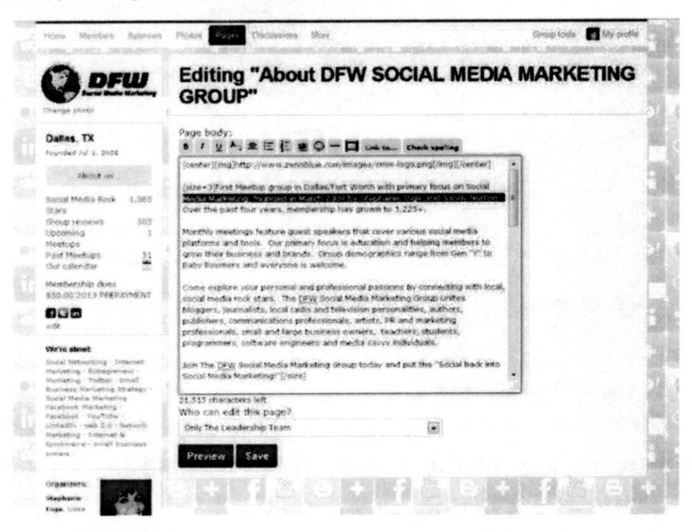

If your video does not show up in the preview at this point, do not worry. To ensure that the video has been added, make sure to click *Submit* at the bottom of the page.

If you'd like to see how the video and Meetup Group description appears to non-members, simply click the *About Us* link in the left column.

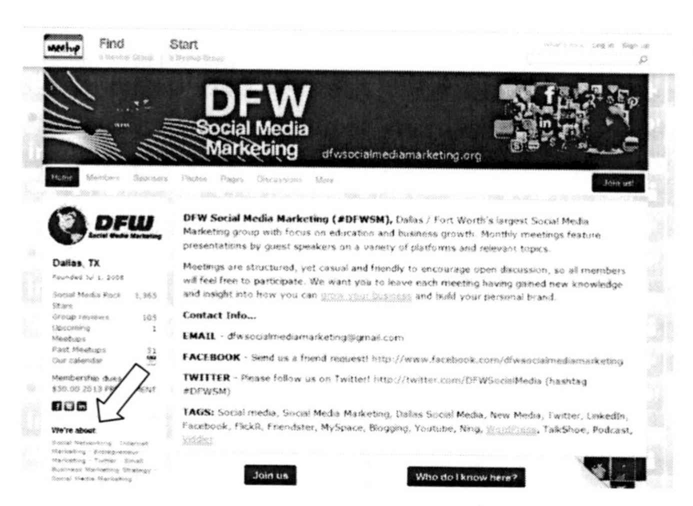

In order to add a video to any page on the Meetup site, you'll need to copy and paste the embedded code for that video to your computer *Clipboard*.

Note: The embed code is not the same as the URL (web address). The embed code will contain a few lines of HTML code created for posting the video to other websites. It's easy to find the appropriate code on the video host website. Once you click the *Share* button, you'll see two options: *Email* and *Embed*.

Right click and copy the embed code to your computer. Paste it into the HTML section of your Meetup group description or the description for a specific Meetup event.

You can also edit your Group description by clicking on *Group Settings* under *Group Tools*, and then click on *Basics*. Make sure that you click *Submit* to save any updates and/or revisions.

Prospective members will see the full expanded description on your Meetup Group home page, above the list of upcoming Meetups.

Existing members of your Meetup Group will see an abbreviated or collapsed version of the group description. Important to note that current members can always read the description by clicking on the *About Us* button in the left column of your Meetup Group home page.

Plan and Schedule Your First Meetup Event!
To bring your Meetup Group to life, it's critical to schedule, list, and announce your first Meetup event as soon as possible. More people will join and attend if they see an event listed on your Meetup calendar.

Choose a Location/Venue
Make a list of basic requirements for your venue. These will vary greatly and depend on the type and/or topic of your Meetup group. Things to consider could be:

- Is the venue suitable for your Meetup group? If your Meetup is a Stay-At-Home-Mom Group, then you wouldn't want to meet at a bar, or then again, maybe you would? Point? Try to pick a venue that is appropriate to your membership.
- How many people do you expect to RSVP and whether everyone will fit comfortably, i.e., what is the venue's seating capacity?
- Is the location convenient for all attendees?
- Is there ample parking and/or public transportation available?
- Is WiFi available? If so, is there a charge? This is more and more important as more people become tech-oriented.
- Will you need a projector and screen for presentations? Perhaps you might have a guest speaker.

Restaurants and coffee shops are very popular and usually a great choice for new Meetup groups since meetings start out casual and fairly small. Some restaurants and venues will be open to offering specials to large groups, so don't be afraid to ask. Most restaurants will be particularly keen on offering a special if your Meetup event is held on a less busy evening. Brand new restaurants may be more willing than an established restaurant since they most likely need business.

- Do they offer a variety of food and beverage choices?
- Will gratuity be included in the check?
- Are they willing to issue individual checks? (This is huge!)
- Check the noise level; you need to be able to hear each other.
- Do they take reservations?
- Do they have private rooms?
- What day of the week would be best for large groups?

Search for the perfect venue. Finding a venue that meets all your criteria may be challenging, so ask friends, members and colleagues for recommendations.

Keep an eye out for *Groupon* (http://www.groupon.com/) and *Living Social* (https://www.livingsocial.com/) specials and other daily deals as this is a good indication that they are willing to work with you. Chain restaurants are not usually as flexible as family-owned, local venues.

What to Do At Your First Meetup Event

Your first Meetup event will be all about introductions and getting to know each other. Keep it simple, stress free, and interesting so you can enjoy it as much as everyone else. You may also want to discuss possible topics for future Meetup events so that people will know what to expect in the way of discussions.

Don't stress out too much about making everything perfect. Everything will fall into place in due time. A great way to help get the conversations going is to plan an icebreaker activity.

Writing an Event Description

All Meetup events require an Event Description. Telling about your first Meetup event is your chance to really convey *just how great* it's going to be. Some things you might want to include:

- What you'll be doing at the Meetup event
- What will it be like
- Will it be an activity, a discussion, or a presentation
- What's the topic of discussion
- Who's presenting and what will they present
- Do members need to bring anything
- Who should come and are newcomers welcome
- Who shouldn't come
- What should a newcomer expect
- How will members benefit from coming to your Meetup event
- How long will the Meetup event last

The more details you provide, the better. The members need this information in order to decide if they'd like to attend.

Meetup event descriptions are designed to help Organizers create a mental image of what the Meetup event will be like for members. Organizers can add photos, links to resources, and/or use basic formatting options to make key information stand out. Here are some recommendations to keep in mind when scheduling your Meetup event, whether it's your first or your future events.

- Keep it simple. Make it easy for members to scan your Meetup content for relevant information.
- Use **bold**, *italics*, or bullets for emphasis. Highlight important details so they stand out.
- Add photos to give members a sense of where you're going and who attends your Meetups. It's an optional feature, but a nice touch when setting expectations for your members.

Choosing a Date and Time

This can be challenging, especially when you're just getting started. Here are some things to keep in mind.

Think about what's most appropriate for your Meetup Group. A wine-tasting Meetup Group is going to have different needs from an eBay Meetup. Decide what time of day your members (or future members) would most likely be available to attend your Meetup events.

Choose a date and time that is convenient for you. If not, it may become too stressful and cause you to get discouraged. It's impossible to know everyone's schedule, so do the best you can based on the demographics of your membership.

As previously stated, Monday, Tuesday, and Wednesday evenings tend to work out well because those are slow days for most possible venues. Keep in mind that Wednesday is church for some people and something to consider when planning your Meetup event. If you're thinking about Sunday afternoon, remember that during football season, many restaurants show the games and advertise heavily to attract sport fans.

Poll your members and ask for their recommendation using Meetup Group email messaging. You can also set up a poll and ask for topic ideas.

Remember that you can't please everyone. Not every member will be able to make every Meetup, and that's alright. The important thing is to get your first Meetup event scheduled and posted on your calendar. You can always change your regular meeting time if you see that the date isn't working as well as you planned.

When it comes to picking a date, give yourself enough time to plan, for people to find you, and to market your event on your favorite social media sites. Three or four weeks from the day you create your Meetup group is more than enough time.

Meetup Topics

Every Meetup Group meeting needs a special, definite topic, or it's just a social gathering and that's alright. As the group organizer, it is your decision, and in the beginning, it's a good idea to keep things simple.

Spend some time checking out other Meetup groups for ideas and not just in your area. You don't have to reinvent the wheel, but again, it's always a good idea to think outside the box. I'm not encouraging anyone to be a copycat, but I do encourage learning from others that have seen success. What are they doing? What topics are they covering?

If your group is an eBay Meetup group, I recommend having a round-table discussion or Powerseller panel twice a year to discuss the spring and fall eBay announcements. There is usually a lot of "scuttlebutt" going around within the eBay community regarding eBay announcements, so this is the perfect opportunity to help answer questions and discuss the new changes. Member-centered discussion-style meetings are a great way to engage your members and make them an integral part of the meeting.

Every once in awhile, brainstorming sessions where members help come up with suggestions for future meetings is a great idea. It is always fun and an excellent way to get members involved. People who get involved tend to feel more connected. This is very conducive to long-term membership and regular attendance.

Popular eBay topics are: packing & shipping, customer service excellence, photography and photo editing, writing great descriptions, reviews & guides, marketing eBay listings using social media, eBay stores, market research tools, third-party listing tools, multi-channel selling (including Amazon). For more ideas, I recommend browsing the *Applications* inside your *My eBay* dashboard.

Another way to enhance your meetings is by inviting guest speakers on a topic of interest to your group. Guest speakers can always be found.

- Keep an eye out for guest speakers everywhere.
- Browse through your member profiles to see if there are any experts for a particular topic.
- Perform targeted searches on: LinkedIn, Twitter, and Facebook.
- Search Google using the *Advanced Search.*
- Poll your members and ask for recommendations.
- Have index cards at the check-in table for speaker and topic recommendations.
- Ask other Meetup organizers for suggestions.

Remember that people attend Meetups for three reasons: education, networking, and fun.

Group Settings

To edit any part of your Meetup group Home page, scroll over *Group Tools* from the navigation bar and click on *Group Settings*.

From there, you'll find options to edit the basic information, mailing list, topics, member and privacy settings, sponsors, plus much, much more!

6 – Your Meetup Group Meetings

Membership Dues

Membership dues are optional and are unrelated to those paid by organizers to Meetup.com to create a Meetup group. There are two options available to organizers when it comes to charging your members: meeting/event entrance fees and your group's membership fee.

Because entrance fees are usually collected at each meeting upon entrance into the venue, it is a good idea to begin this practice from the first meeting. Whether to go on to charge general membership dues once your group is established is your decision as Meetup Organizer. Membership dues are typically collected once a month or once a year.

These funds will help to offset your monthly subscription to Meetup.com, gifts for guest speakers, venue rental, refreshments, printing, name tags, holiday events, etc. It is much easier to start off charging nominal membership fees, rather than later switching from free membership to adding this fee.

Recording Membership Dues

If a member chooses to pay their dues through the Meetup home page by clicking *Pay Online,* the money collected via the online payment options will automatically populate in your group's *Money Tab.* If a member pays you directly with cash or check, you will want to record the payments manually.

To record payments manually, scroll over *Group Tools,* click *Money* and, under *All Transactions,* select *Record a Payment Received.* Next click *Membership Dues* from the drop-down menu, and begin typing the member's name. Select his/her profile from the drop-down menu, enter the date of the payment, the amount collected, and *Submit.* This will add the payment to your Meetup group's *Money* page.

To Charge Event Fees

You can use *Amazon Payments* or *PayPal* to collect event fees through your Meetup.

To set your event so that an event fee is displayed:

1. Go to Meetup.com (http://www.meetup.com/) and log into your account.
2. Go to the home page of the Meetup group.
3. Click the name of the Meetup that you want to change.
4. Click *Edit.*
5. When asked if you will be *"Charging for this Meetup?",* select *"Yes, I'd like to charge my members."*

   There are several available payment options:

   - Payment is not required to RSVP
   - Payment is required to RSVP
   - Payment at the door or by some other means of your choice

   Leaders/Organizers can also choose to accept credit cards via *PayPal Here* or *Square.*

   PayPal Here^{tm} (https://www.paypal.com/webapps/mpp/credit-card-reader)**:** Get paid anywhere. Accept credit cards, checks and PayPal wherever your customers are on your iPhone, iPad, or Android devices with *PayPal Here*^{tm}, 2.7% per transaction. Get FREE card reader and app.

   Square (http://www.squaredup.com/)**:** Start accepting credit cards today, 2.75% per swipe and next day deposit. Get free card reader and app at SquareUp.com.

6. You can choose your refund policy, or uncheck the box if you choose not to issue refunds.
7. Scroll to the bottom of the page and click *Change Details*

Viewing Received Payments

To see all of the payments you've received, click on *Payments Received* within your *Account* page. You'll get a quick overview of all the payments.

You can choose whether or not you want to look at just Meetup Events, Membership Dues, or Sponsorships by clicking on any one of those tabs on the page.

Under the *Membership Dues* tab, clicking on the name of your Meetup Group will show you all of the dues you've received, individually by members.

On the *Meetup Events* tab, clicking on the name of a particular event will show you all of the payment details for that particular Meetup Event.

Marking a Member as Paid

If you're collecting payments for a Meetup Event, your Members' payment status (whether they've paid or not) will appear next to their name on the right side of your Meetup Event's page. (The paid or unpaid status is only shown to Organizers.)

If a member pays via PayPal or Amazon Payments, their payment status will automatically update from Unpaid to Paid.

If you're collecting payment by cash or check at the door, you'll need to update their status manually. However, it is important to note that while this is optional, it is a convenient way for you to keep up with attendance and funds collected.

It's simple to do. Navigate to the Meetup *event page* and under *Attending* on the right hand side, find the member who paid, and click *Mark Paid* next to their name.

You will be asked to enter more information about their payment. Then, click *Add Payment* to save the changes.

Check-In At A Meetup Event

The leadership of the group should have a check-in table ready at the entrance to each meeting. The check-in table is the first point of contact with attendees, provides a place to hand out name tags, door prize tickets, collect entry fees (if applicable), display marketing materials, handouts, or sponsor-related materials.

In addition to the traditional check-in, members can also check in on their favorite social media sites. These check-ins provide a quick way to update or give a shout out to the Organizer and members who have RSVP'd to the Meetup. Others will know who and when each member arrives at the meeting, but you as the Organizer will be able to track attendance. Meetup.Com Resources (discussed later) offers several aids to help you prepare for your members arriving at each meeting.

Meetup Mobile App

Currently, the Meetup App is available for iPhone and Android devices. Check-in begins 30 minutes before the scheduled start of a Meetup and cuts off three hours after it began.

Once the Meetup is ready to start, each member will see a green box that reads*, At this Meetup?* When they check in, it tells everyone they're here! Click *Check-in to this Meetup* and they're done!

Don't forget that members can also add a comment to let everyone know if they're running late, if they can't find the venue, or if they just want to say, "Hi!"

Foursquare

Discover and share cool places with friends, family, and associates. As of this date, more than 30 million people are registered with Foursquare and are checking in all over the globe. Discover and learn about new places near-by, find any type of food that you might be craving, earn badges, and even become the mayor of your favorite establishment.

Facebook

To check into a location, make sure you've enabled location services on your smart phone, and follow these instructions:

1. Open your News Feed.
2. Tap the blue location icon to *Check In.*
3. Choose a place or type in the name of the place in the search bar.
4. Write a caption, tag friends, and/or add a photo.

Automating Daily, Weekly, Monthly Tasks

All members of your Meetup leadership team have the ability to schedule the regularly recurring Meetup events for the group.

Start by scheduling the first Meetup in the series the same way you would schedule any Meetup. Click on *Group Tools* and select *Schedule a Meetup* from the drop-down list. You can also choose to repeat an already-scheduled Meetup event by going to the *Event Detail* page and choose the *Edit* link if it's an upcoming Meetup or *Copy* if it's a past Meetup.

In *schedule* or *edit* within the Meetup page, you'll see a section labeled *Automatically Repeat This Meetup*. Expand that section and choose how often you'd like your Meetup to repeat. You can set it to repeat by days, weeks, or months.

If you'd like your series to end at a certain point, click on *Change* next to *Stop Repeating* in order to enter an end date.

Meetup makes it difficult to mess up because they also let you choose whether or not to receive an automatic reminder a few days before each Meetup. Within this reminder, you can review your Meetup announcement before it is sent in order to make any needed changes, tweaks, and additions.

Always remember to fill in all details about your Meetup. Once you've finished, click the *Schedule Meetup Now* link located at the bottom of the page. After that, you'll see all of your automatically repeated Meetups on the calendar.

Reminders and Personalized Emails

As an Organizer, it's up to you whether you'd like the Meetup site to send automatic reminders for upcoming Meetup events on the calendar to your members.

For Meetup Groups with one or two Meetup events each month, the reminders can be a very effective way to get members to RSVP. For Groups with several monthly Meetup events, automatic reminders for every single event could be overwhelming.

As Organizer, it's your decision as to whether you think the reminders are appropriate or not. Either way, it's a good idea to send regular email reminders to the members of your group.

Organizers who regularly communicate with their members have more active Meetup groups.

Communicating with your group is easy. Scroll over *Group tools* on your group's home page, click *Email Members,* compose your message, and finally click *Submit*.

An occasional, personalized email to remind folks of upcoming Meetup events, discussing future plans, or asking for suggestions is a fantastic way to keep your members connected, happy, and involved.

7 – Customize Your Meetup Site to Stand Out

Appearance Settings

As a Meetup Organizer, you can customize the look and feel of your Meetup Group's site using the *Appearance* settings under *Group Tools.*

Meetup offers a pre-set menu of complementary color palettes from which to choose. You can also customize the banner or background image on your Meetup page for an even more unique look.

Choose a Color Palette

Choose from one of the preset color palettes to customize your Meetup site and help it stand out.

Meetup's color palettes have complementary color schemes to make it easy to find the right mix of colors for your Meetup group's theme.

Customize your Banner

Make the name of your Meetup Group really pop! Edit your name using the *Basic Info* option under *Group Settings*. The name will automatically be centered, and the letters will expand or contract for the perfect fit.

You can also create a custom banner and save it as an image file. Once it's saved, upload it to your Meetup page. The optimal banner size is 960 pixels x 160 pixels. Again, I use the following tools: *Play With Pictures* by Vertus, *Picasa*, and *Paint*. Important to note that if you're already comfortable with a particular image-editing program, I highly recommend sticking with what you know.

Upload Background Image

Organizers can create a custom background for their Meetup site by uploading a photo using the Meetup toolbar. The settings offer Organizers the option to stretch, tile, or center the background photo.

Create Your Own Color Palette

If you're a web-savvy Meetup designer, you can make your own custom color scheme, and add hex color codes to the preset settings manually. Here is a website to choose your own color combination: http://www.colorcombos.com.

Add HTML To Spruce Up Your Meetup Group's Description!

A Meetup Group's headline and description are two of the most important elements that potential members look at when deciding whether or not they are going to join a group. To help Organizers customize their group's home page, Meetup has made it easier to edit your group's headline and description. You can also add HTML to the group's description, which is a fairly new feature, so be sure and take advantage!

As an organizer, scroll over the group description or headline until you see an *edit* button.

When editing the group description, the interface conveniently displays how it will appear as you edit. For a bit more control, click the *HTML* button and switch to directly edit the HTML code. For eBayers, this is very similar to the description box in the *eBay Sell Your Item Form*.

Create cool, exciting, and inviting pages to give potential members a better understanding of what your group is all about. Effort on the finer details will typically be a good indicator of a well-managed, fun Meetup group. Basic formatting options are available, including *bold* and *font size*. Use these features to emphasize important sentences, link to important pages, or add photos telling your Meetup story.

You can add most HTML tags related to basic layout; however, they currently strip out table and DIV tags, as well as script tags (and class and style attributes). Only Organizers and Co-Organizers can edit the headline and group description.

Changing Your Meetup Group's Web Address (URL)

To change your Meetup group's web address, you'll want to go to the Meetup group's home page, scroll over *Group Tools* and click on *Group Settings*. Click on *Basics* then scroll to the *Where* section and find *Web Address*. Enter the desired web address in the field (6 character minimum), and the system will check to see if it's available for use. Once you've got a valid, available address chosen, click *Submit* to save the changes.

Add Live Streaming Video To Your Meetup Home Page

Not everyone can make it to your Meetup, but with live streaming video, they can follow along from your home page.

It's pretty simple: Meetup is now supporting *UStream*, *Livestream*, and *Slideshare* (for sharing slides from presentations at Meetups). You can also stream live Meetups using *Google+ Hangouts On Air* that are recorded and stored on your YouTube channel. Read more about Google+ *Hangouts* in the chapter on Marketing and Promoting Your Meetup Group.

You can plug the embedded code into the video module on your group's home page. Then, you record the video through whichever site works best for you, and folks looking at your Group's home page will be able to follow along live.

Add, Edit, and Remove Pages

Custom pages provide a space for you to build additional content for your Meetup Group. Use them to create a variety of pages (group policies, video library of past Meetups, group cookbook, alumni page, leadership team bios, frequently asked questions, or anything else that you think would be interesting).

It's always a good idea to create a Frequently Asked Questions Page, once you have received numerous emails from members. This will help save time and frustration from having to repeat the same answers over and over.

Your *About* page is public to everyone who visits your Meetup group site. You can set viewing and editing permissions for all other pages on your group site.

Include as much information as possible about your Meetup group on the *About* page and update it often. It's good practice to mention your *About* page in the welcome email sent to new members.

To edit custom pages, click on the corresponding *Pages* tab from your Meetup Group home page. Make sure you're logged onto your Meetup account. Navigate to the *Edit This Page* link at the top. The menu pop-up will allow you to edit and customize the content. You are also able to add videos and images from this menu.

The *Add A Page* option will allow you to add additional pages to your group Meetup site. You'll see a drop-down menu for setting viewing and editing permissions. Please note that you can only set additional pages to the private setting. In other words, only members of your Meetup will be able to see your additional pages. For example, The Dallas eBaybes & eMales Meetup page has an additional page created for a joint online cookbook. Members can contribute their favorite recipes.

To delete a Page, click on *Pages* in the navigation bar. Scroll down to the bottom to see the *Table of Contents*. Click on the page that you'd like to delete. Once on the page you'd like to delete, look under the page's title. Click *Delete page* and follow the prompts to complete the page's deletion. Your group's landing page, *About* page, is the only page that cannot be deleted

Create a Group Logo

Brand recognition is "all the buzz" these days. One simple way to accomplish this is to have a logo. I have purchased custom logos on eBay for as little as $5.95, and the one we have

today was designed by one of our members. We ran a logo-creating contest during the early days of our group; the winner had the honor of seeing their creation on all of our Meetup pages and printing.

Upload Files To Your Meetup Group

To upload a file to your Meetup Group, scroll over *More* and then click on *Files*. Next, click *Add a File* to select the file from your computer.

You'll have the option to designate who is able to view the file. Choose *Anyone*, *Only Members of the Group*, or *Only the Leadership Team.* Remember that your leadership team consists of the organizer, co-organizers, and assistant organizers.

Maximum file size is 10 MB with a maximum of 100 MB of file storage for each Meetup group.

8 - Adding / Uploading / Sharing Photographs

Members are encouraged to upload and share edited photos to the Meetup site and *Facebook* fan page after the events. Here are some guidelines for doing this.

Please don't upload every photo, only those that have been edited. Pick and choose the best ones to share. Share them by using the 'Photos' tab on the event page.

Meetup allows each member to upload 50 photographs, but imagine if everyone uploaded the maximum number. It would be information overload, and take forever for people to browse through the album.

Make sure that photos are right-side-up before uploading. It's very irritating to look at pictures that are sideways or upside down. *Picasa* is a free image-editing software tool from *Google* and super simple to use. I highly recommend downloading a free copy and giving it a test drive.

You can include links in the photo comment box if you have the photos stored on a third-party site such as

- *Shutterfly* (http://www.shutterfly.com/)
- *Photobucket* (http://photobucket.com/)
- *Flickr* (http://www.flickr.com/)
- *Picasa* or
- *Facebook*

Don't upload blurry photos.

Organizers have the ability to delete photos that are inappropriate, blurry, repetitive, or unflattering.

9 – Share Your Meetup With the World

Your Meetup Group's Web Presence!

Now your Meetup Group can prominently display its related social networks and web links.

Does your Meetup Group have a *Facebook* group or fan page? How about a group *Twitter* handle or hashtag? How about a *LinkedIn* group? Does your Meetup group have a blog on *Tumblr* or elsewhere?

(A hashtag is a word or a phrase prefixed with the symbol #. Short messages and social networking sites such as Twitter or Instagram use hashtags to provide a means of grouping such messages since one can search for the hashtag and get the set of messages that contain it.)

Announce your Meetup events in the appropriate category on *Craigslist*. This is a very effective method of reaching the local audience.

Display all of the social media icons on your Meetup Group pages to encourage members to connect with you and those sites also.

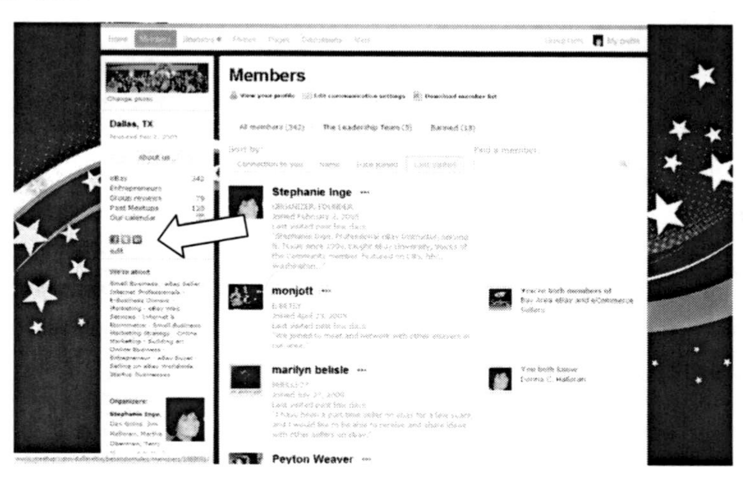

Many Meetup Groups already have a presence on these social media sites. This can be a great way to promote your group as well as connect with individual members in creative ways.

Organizers and Co-Organizers can set these up by clicking *Add/edit your group's links* in the box on the left side of any group page, or by looking under *Optional Features* in Group Settings.

Meetup provides a plethora of useful marketing tools; however, a quick Google search will turn up an endless array of free marketing tools. I recommend that you check several of them out and do not just rely on the ones provided by Meetup.

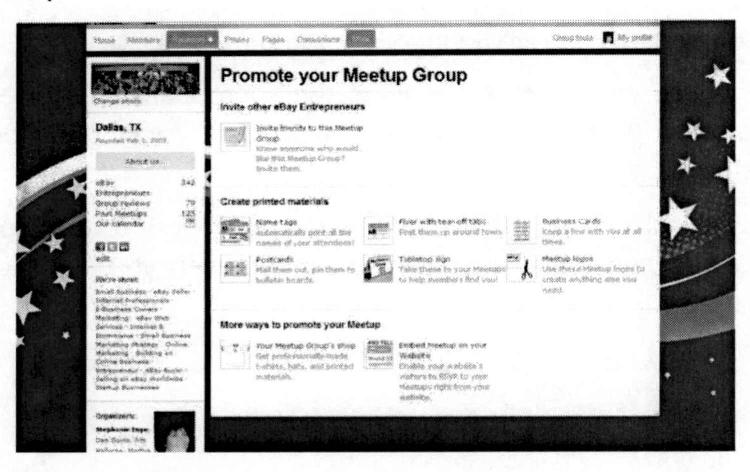

As Organizer, there are several options to invite your friends. You can import your contacts from Yahoo or Gmail or you can type an email address directly into the appropriate box. I highly recommend including a short, personalized message if you import from your contacts so they'll know it came from you and isn't spam.

You can also embed a Meetup widget on your website or blog. You can create a Pinterest page for your Meetup Group and include a link to your Meetup site in your profile. Here are some ideas for naming your Pin Boards that may work for you depending on the type of Meetup Group you create: A-Listers, Events, Leadership Team, Infographics, Blogs, Tips, Tricks & Best Practices, Video Tutorials, Alumni, Members, etc.

For the Pinterest naysayers, it is the fourth highest traffic generator on the Internet, behind Google, YouTube, and Facebook, and therefore, it is a fabulous way to increase visibility for your Meetup Group.

Social media is paramount to the success of your Meetup Group. Create a Facebook fan page for your group and decide whether to make it public or private. There's no right or wrong way to do this.

Create a cool, descriptive timeline cover for your Facebook page using your favorite image-editing tool. The dimensions for a Facebook Timeline Cover are 851 x 315 pixels. You will need this.

We all know that Google is the "Big Kahuna", so if you really want to ramp things up, create a Google+ page for your

Meetup Group. The Google search robots will be all over it in no time!

Create a Google+ cover photo for your group. The dimensions are massive, 2120 x 1192 pixels. This gives you lots of room for branding your Meetup Group.

I use various tools to create cover photos and banners. It really just depends on my mood and the look I'm trying to achieve. My favorites are *Play With Pictures* by Vertus, *Picasa* by Google, and *Paint* by Microsoft. I'm no graphic artist, and you don't have to be either. Anyone can create a really cool cover photo with the help of a few inexpensive and/or free tools.

Add *Google Analytics* to your Meetup site. It's very easy and no technical expertise is required. (See Resources.)

If your Meetup group is business- or tech-related, create a LinkedIn group to mirror the other social media groups you've created. It all boils down to maximum visibility and search engine optimization.

Printed Material

Meetup provides templates for various printed material, including name tags, flyers, postcards, tabletop signs and business cards, which makes it super simple to brand your group and create professional advertising and marketing materials.

Create A Meetup Store!

Meetup has partnered with Zazzle.com to make it super simple to create and sell branded merchandise for your Meetup Group. Create a Zazzle store to sell the merchandise with a few clicks of your mouse. What a cool idea and a wonderful way to brand your Meetup group. You can have a shop up and running in no time at no extra charge to you.

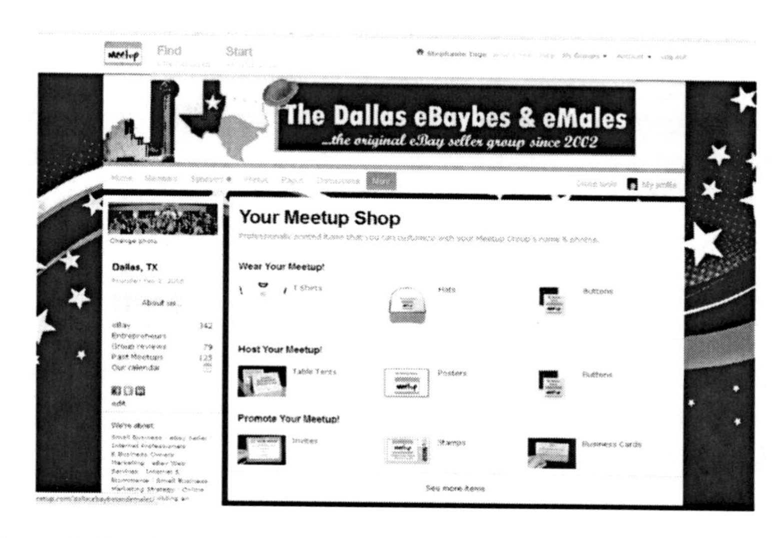

Search Engine Optimization For Your Meetup Group

Good, rich content is the key to improving your search ranking with search engines such as *Google, Bing, Yahoo* and others. Search Engine Optimization (SEO) for your Meetup Group is so, so important. Make sure that your Meetup pages have interesting and relevant information that is updated often. If not, search-engine bots will overlook your Meetup pages.

Here are a few suggestions for things you can do to make sure you're providing interesting and useful information about your Meetup group.

Include Location and Main Topic In Your Meetup Group's Name

Cute acronyms and clever names might sound cool, but for the purpose of search engine optimization, the perfect group name should be simple and reflect the topic of your group.

Perfect formula for naming your Meetup Group, according to Meetup.com:

Location + One or two descriptive words + Meetup

Include a summary sentence at the beginning of your Group description.

The first sentence should be very short and provide a simple explanation of what your Meetup Group is about. By short, they mean around 100 characters - "We are eBay sellers who meet once a month at Canyon Creek Country Club to discuss eBay and all things related to ecommerce." That's it!

This will help search engine users quickly understand what clicking on the link to your Meetup Group will take them to. You don't want folks to be confused.

Freshen up your group description with good, descriptive details. The rest of your Meetup Group description should include details about who should join the group, why they should join, what they can expect, and what sort of things your group does.

Remember, don't write a novel. Make sure you've got relevant information in there, but don't go overboard. You can always add or revise the description later if necessary.

Extra bonus points – link to your Meetup group from other sites on the Internet.

One thing search engine robots use in determining whether a website is useful is checking to see if *other* websites are linking to it. These are called "backlinks". Post a link to your Meetup Group from your blog or get friends and members to link to your Meetup group from their websites.

Warning from Meetup: Repetitive content, 'non-human language', and other deceptive tactics designed to trick the search engines can get your Meetup group de-listed and removed from the search results. That goes for search engines as well as the search functions on the Meetup site.

10 – Broadcast Your Live Meetup Event

With a few simple steps and no techie experience at all, you can broadcast your Meetup event live via streaming video with nothing more than a laptop, provided it has a built-in video camera/webcam to film the event. Eventually, you may want to purchase a USB microphone for the laptop to get crisp, professional audio, but it's not mandatory.

In addition to the event being live, streaming via the Internet, it is being recorded on YouTube for viewing later. This is all accomplished using Google+ Hangouts On Air.

Create an event on your Google+ page and create a banner or use one of the freebies provided by Google+.

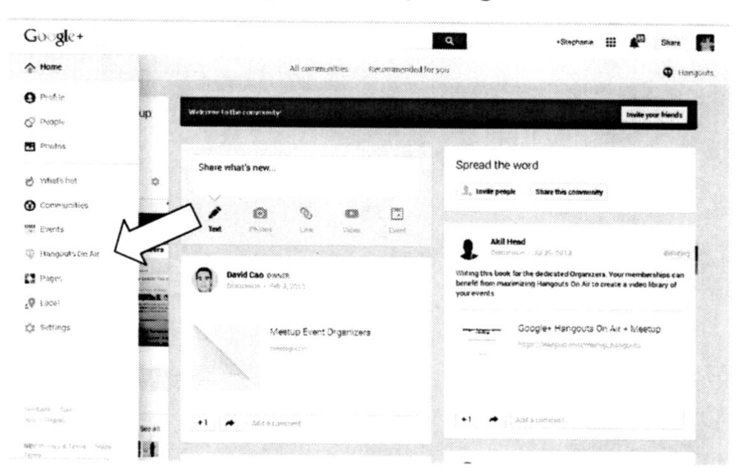

When you're ready to start the live broadcast, you'll click on the *Hangouts On Air* link (on the left, below the *Events* link) to begin streaming the event live via YouTube and your Google+ page. You'll receive a URL for your broadcast, which you will then copy and paste into the appropriate box. Go to your event page and click on *Details*.

After clicking the down-arrow inside the *Details* box, you'll see the following drop-down menu:

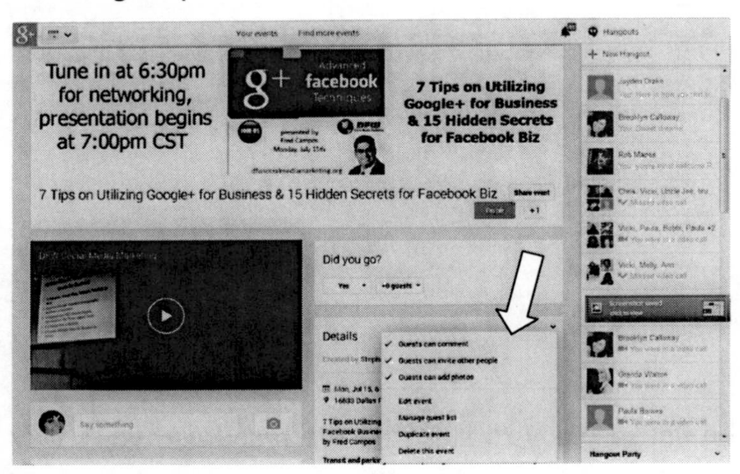

Click on *Edit Event* to navigate to the next screen:

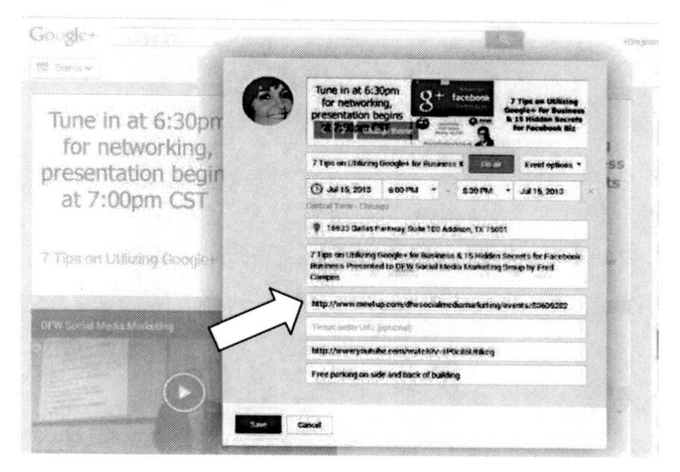

Copy and paste the YouTube link for your live event into the box shown by the arrow, then click *Save*. If you'd like the live event (*Hangout on Air*) to also be streamed on your website or Meetup event page, copy and paste that URL into the other box, as shown above.

11 – Best Practices for Meetup Organizers

A *best practice* is a method or technique that has consistently shown best results and can even evolve to become better as improvements are discovered. It is also used to describe the process of developing and following a standard way of doing things that multiple organizations can use. The best practices described here are for your benefit in making your group the best that it can be.

This chapter addresses you, the Organizer, personally. If you wish your Meetup Group to succeed, first determine why you should organize a Meetup! The best reason for starting a Meetup group is simple. You should do it because you enjoy helping, you enjoy networking, and you would like to build a community of like-minded individuals.

The absolute worst taboo for a Meetup organizer is to have an ulterior motive for wanting to start a group. It is against Meetup policy to start a Meetup Group for the purpose of selling services, products, or self-promotion.

It's natural for new organizers to try hard to please everyone and ask for input from members, but I have a warning for you. When you ask for input from ten different people, you'll get ten different answers; therefore, my advice is to research your questions and/or Google to find an answer.

Keep your feelers out for members who may potentially desire to join your leadership team for all the right reasons. Ask them if they'd be interested in a role as *Assistant Organizer* or *Co-*

Organizer. Once you enlist the help of one or two members, plan an informal production meeting to discuss possible topics and potential guest speakers.

If your group is brand new, plan your first meeting as soon as possible. If you're an experienced Meetup Organizer/Leader, plan a committee meeting in October or November to start planning for the upcoming year. Make a list of possible guest speakers and topics. Peruse your list of members and their profiles to find potential speakers. I also recommend doing a targeted search on LinkedIn.

Another way to come up with interesting topics is to create an online poll. Ask members to vote on a list of topics or have them recommend some. You can also ask members if they'd be willing to speak on a particular topic or teach an upcoming class. Get members involved! Note, asking members for topic interest is not like asking members for feedback. Keeping your members involved and inspired is one thing; asking everyone for their opinions on the group is entirely different.

Remember that you are the Group Leader and Organizer; however, that doesn't mean that your members want you as the featured speaker at every single meeting. That is likely a recipe for disaster and surefire quick way to decrease your membership. Every now and then is perfectly acceptable.

For most business/tech-type Meetup groups, a blend of networking, education, and Q & A work very well. Food and beverage will never hurt. This is the precise reason that restaurants are the perfect choice for a meeting venue. Always remember to mix fun with business in order to keep things interesting. There are several meeting formats that work well: round table discussion, panel discussion, guest speaker, class, and/or workshop.

If you have a large number of members, then you may be able to find speakers within your group. Searching on LinkedIn will really open up a wide range of speakers and topics. Don't be shy about asking once you feel their profile fits the topic you have chosen for your Meetup.

Try not to repeat the same topic or speaker more than once a year. Once a speaker has agreed to speak on a particular topic, ask them to send you a brief outline of their presentation. This way, you will have a better idea what to expect. You never want to have a speaker that ends up doing a one-hour infomercial on their business, product, or themselves. Talk about a recipe for disaster! It's perfectly acceptable for them to mention their business, their book, or their product at the end of their presentation, but it should never be about self-promotion. Make sure to discuss this with your speakers in advance.

Add each event to your Meetup calendar and include the agenda. Ask speakers to send a headshot, logo, list of discussion topics, brief bio, business information, and link to their website. When creating the announcement for the Meetup, include the link to the guest speaker's website and detailed information about the venue for the meeting. Include this information on your Meetup event page, as well.

Set up an account on *Twitter*, *Foursquare*, and *Google+*. Also create a *Facebook* fan page. Be sure to tweet and post about your events at least every couple days. You want to help get the largest and best audience possible for your speaker, presenter and/or panel participants.

Create a *Twitter* hashtag for your Meetup Group. My Meetup hashtags are *#DALLASEBAYBES* and *#DFWSM*. Create a handout for each meeting that includes the hashtag, speaker information, and presentation outline. Include a Call-To-Action (CTA) that asks your members to tweet about the event and encourages your members to "check in" on *Facebook* and *Foursquare.*

Offer a one-month free sponsorship on your Meetup site for your guest speakers as an incentive and token of appreciation.

Send out personalized emails to your members in advance of your Meetup events. Nobody likes a form letter, so take a moment to add that personal touch. Include a CTA at the end of your email that asks members to help spread some "social media love" by posting announcements about the upcoming event on their favorite social media sites. A CTA could and should also include an RSVP. Include your hashtag and link to your Meetup Facebook fan page.

Be sure to send a thank you card or email to your guest speaker the following day. This really means a lot to them and illustrates professionalism.

When deciding on a guest speaker, it's easier to focus on local people rather than nationally known speakers unless you know that person will be in town attending a conference or trade show. Many speakers like to make the most out of a business trip, so they might welcome your request for them to speak.

Remember that meetings need to have value and be fun; otherwise, your attendance may begin to dwindle.

On occasion, think about partnering with other local Organizers to have a joint Meetup with groups who share similar interest. For example, *DFW Wordpress, DFW Social Media Marketing,* and/or *DFW SEO/SEM Group* combine meetings on occasion.

Once your group is established (3 - 6 meetings), you'll want to charge a modest cover charge/entrance fee of $3.00 to $10.00. Most people are quick to click "Yes" on the RSVP page if they don't have any skin in the game; however, if there is a fee to get in, they will normally think twice. Charging a nominal fee increases your membership to more serious members, and your RSVP no-show list will decrease.

Many people who join and attend your first few meetings may disappear, but don't lose hope. People are human. They get busy and sometimes forget; it's not you, so don't take it personally. Don't give up hope on anyone or assume that they won't be back. I've actually had people thank me for not giving up on them. They have told me how much they appreciate that I kept them in the loop.

If you know someone is a new member and attending your Meetup for the first time, try to make them feel welcome. If time permits, introduce them to a few members who are friendly, outgoing, and will make them feel comfortable. This is key to keeping them coming back. Remember that we all want to feel like we belong.

Don't over-extend yourself by trying to organize more than two Meetup groups. You'll spread yourself too thin and start to feel overwhelmed. Keep things simple, stress-free and interesting!

As for location, try to find something that is centrally located. "*Central to who?"* is always the question of the day. Just use your best judgment. A downtown location is almost never a good idea. Traffic and parking are issues difficult to overcome in a downtown location. If you're meeting in the evening, after work, you'll want something that is located near one or two major thoroughfares. This will make it as convenient as possible to get to in rush hour traffic.

Consistency is very important! Decide on a specific date, time, and location, and stick to it. People are creatures of habit. They will begin to look forward to the monthly meetings and mark their calendars accordingly. Once you've scheduled a meeting, don't ever cancel it, unless it is a dire emergency.

Joining other Meetup Groups to use them as an opportunity to promote your group is a big "no-no". Don't do it. Plastering links to your events on their comments page or Facebook fan page is annoying. If you do join another group for self-promotion, do so by networking with individuals on an individual basis. Don't just show up and hand out a stack of business cards or flyers for your group. If you plan to do that, always, always, always ask the Organizer for permission first. To do any less would be unprofessional and downright rude. Remember the "Golden Rule" and try to follow it always.

12 – Best Practices for Meetup Members

Best Practices

The best practices described here are for your benefit in making your group the best that it can be. These apply to you, the Organizer, as well as to each of your members.

Create a complete profile when you join any Meetup Group. Make sure to upload a profile picture and not a logo or photo of your pet. The purpose of the profile picture is for people to recognize you when you attend meetings. Hopefully, you won't be bringing your pet, so post a picture of yourself.

Equally as important, use your real name. Do not use the name of your business. When you meet someone new, do you introduce yourself as, "Sally's Secret Treasures," or "Sally Smith?" You get the point, right?

Avoid cheesy titles such as Johnny the-Get-Rich-Quick-Guy. That is such a turn-off. Ask yourself; do you like being around a blow-hard when you're at a cocktail party? Probably not.

If you'd like to be helpful and get involved with a Meetup Group, the first thing to remember is to always RSVP. This helps the group organizer plan for the meeting. Organizers really appreciate members who take the time do this. The earlier you RSVP, the better. They need to know who's attending the Meetup as well as the number of guests to expect.

If you RSVP 'yes' to a Meetup, please honor that RSVP! If something comes up and you can't attend, be courteous and respectful by logging in and changing your RSVP to 'no.' Do not email the Organizer to tell them you can't make it. This just creates more work for them.

Help spread the word about the Meetup on your favorite social media sites, and make sure to add a link to the event page. Next to an RSVP, this is the most important thing you could do to help your organizer.

Honoring an RSVP and attending regular Meetup events are the most important part of being a member in good standing. Meetup will delete members who become inactive.

Once you arrive at the Meetup, there are several ways to check-in via social media: Meetup Mobile App, Facebook, and Foursquare

Most Organizers work very hard to plan their Meetup events, and many can use a helping hand. If you'd like to help, the best thing to do is ask. Even if you don't see yourself as an Assistant Organizer, there's probably something you can do to help.

How about offering to take and edit photos of the Meetups? Do you know of a great venue? Are you good at designing flyers or handouts for the Meetup events? How about offering to add a link for the Meetup event to your website? All these suggestions may seem trivial, but they're all important and could really help make a big difference.

If you need to email the Organizer about a particular event or topic, include the name of the event or topic in the email subject line.

If you feel like you're receiving too many email reminders, log in to your Meetup account and adjust your email preferences. Since Meetup is virtually completely automated, adjusting your preferences is more appropriate than emailing the Organizer to complain. With that said, don't complain that you didn't know about an event or receive notification if you have made the decision to turn off your email reminders.

13 – Meetup.com Resources for Organizers

Attendance Tool

The attendance tool provides Organizers a quick way to keep track of who attended a Meetup event.

Organizers have a quick and easy way to filter members by Attendance, RSVP, or name: a *Didn't Attend* option that can be used to indicate excused absences

To check it out, simply click *Edit Attendance* on any past Meetup.

Track your Meetup Group Using Google Analytics

Meetup provides organizers with the ability to track visitors, traffic, and page views to your Meetup group. Meetup has made it simple for your Meetup groups you to interface with Google's free Analytics platform.

Google Analytics will provide you with all sorts of information. Learn your page view count, the location of your visitors, most popular pages, high/low traffic times, and much more. See which Meetups gets the most traffic. You can even tell if your emails are effective in driving folks to your site. Studying what words people search to find your Meetup is the most fascinating, helpful, and useful feature. This will help you write a compelling group description by using the tags for your Meetup group more effectively.

Setting up Google Analytics is easy and painless. It's especially easy if you already have a Gmail account. If not, you'll need to create a Google account first and then sign up for Google Analytics. Get the special tracking code from Google Analytics, and then input that code into your Meetup group's group settings. Next, you'll want to go to www.google.com/analytics and click *Sign Up*.

You'll see the following page that contains several fields:

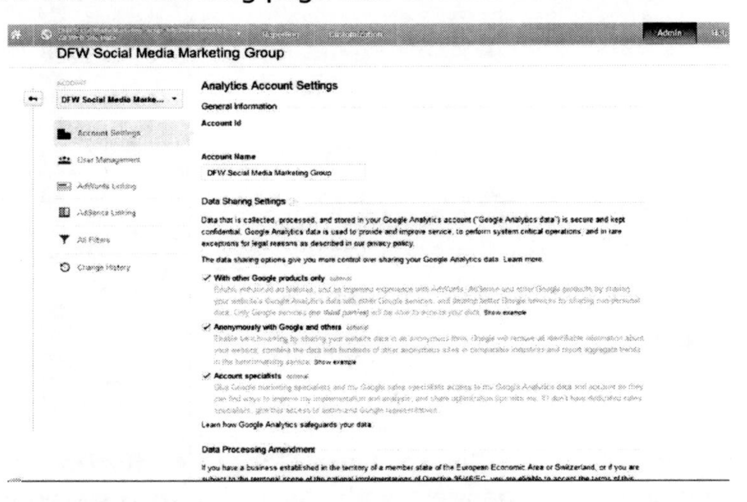

Be sure to enter the web address (the URL) of your Meetup group, i.e., www.meetup.com/yourgroup/. Make certain you include the final forward slash. Make sure to also include an account name, your time zone country, your time zone, the account name, and *Data Sharing* settings.

When you're all set, hit *Get Tracking ID link*, accept the user agreement, and your *Tracking ID* will be on the next page. It will look similar to UA-12345678-1.

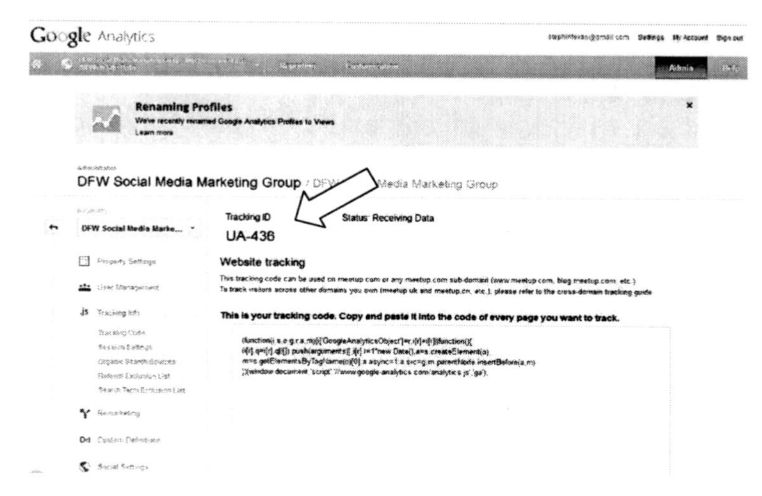

Copy the entire *Tracking ID*, and then go to back to your Meetup group's home page. The only number you need is the UA number since the extra code has already been installed. Again, from your Meetup group home page, scroll over the *Group Tools* link, click *Group Settings* and go to *Optional Features*, where you'll find a section for *Google Analytics*.

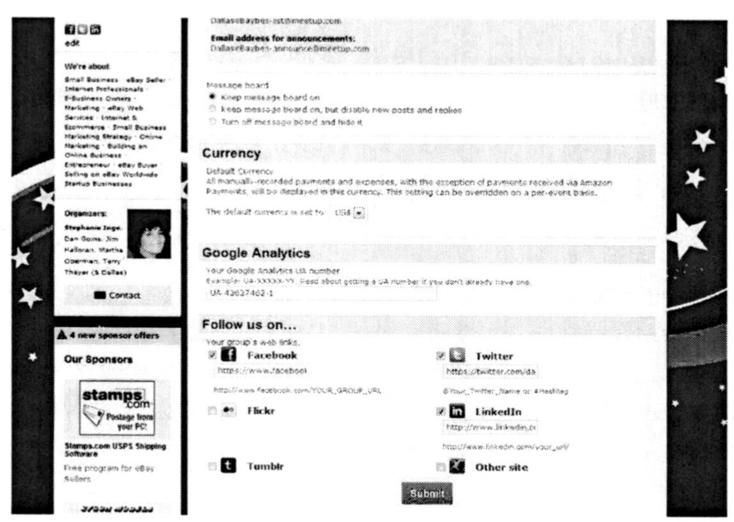

Enter your *UA code*, and hit *Submit* and you're all set! Now you can use *Google Analytics* to start learning about who's visiting your Meetup group. Keep in mind Google Analytics most often requires twenty-four hours to report information.

Automatic Name Tags

There is an easy way to automatically print name tags for everyone attending a Meetup event. Name tags can have a surprisingly large impact at your Meetup events. With pre-printed tags, it's much easier to break the ice, get to know attendees, facilitate conversation, and make newcomers more comfortable. As an added bonus, nametags make it easier as an organizer to remember everyone.

To print name tags, follow these simple steps:

- Hover mouse over the *More* tab within the navigation bar to view the drop-down menu.
- From the drop-down menu, click the *Promote* link.
- On the next page you will click on the *Name Tags* link inside the *Create Printed Materials* section.

From Meetup.com:

A note about printing:

> *This page is sized to fit Avery name tag labels #8395, #5395, or #45395. Or, use regular paper and cut out the name tags to insert them into plastic holders.*
>
> *You'll need Adobe's free Acrobat Reader to download and print name tags.*

You have the option to include the name of your Meetup Group on the tags and have the ability to edit the name from the *Print Name Tag* screen. Other options include printing with regular ink or low ink and what information to include on the tags (member name, photo, and title or role).

Once this information has been selected, click on the red *Create Name Tags* button, located at the bottom of the page. Voilà!

Printable RSVP list

Print the RSVP list for your Meetup event and use it to check people in. This makes life a lot easier on the day of the event.

Here's the process:

- Go to *Print RSVPs* under *Who's Coming.*
- Sort by member *Name* or *RSVP Type.*
- If you asked members questions when they "RSVP'd", you may choose to show or hide those answers when you print.
- Choose whether or not to hide photos and the Meetup description when you print.
- View member comments and how many guests they're bringing.

Message Boards: Discussion View and Forum View

The default view for each message board forum is *Discussion View*. It's easy to change the message board to *Forum View* by scrolling over the *Discussions* link. Next, click on the *Message Board* link and from there, click on *Change to Forum View*.

The *Forum View* window allows you to group related discussions into different forums. In *Forum View*, you can create up to 20 different forums, move discussions from one forum to another, edit or delete forums, and arrange them any way you like.

In *Forum View*, Organizers and Assistant Organizers can select privacy levels for each forum. Privacy options can be set to allow only group members, organizers only, or everyone (even non-group members).

If you've changed to Forum View, you can always go back to the Discussion View. Just click on *Change to Discussion View* link.

Keep in mind that only Organizers can change to *Forum View* and back to Discussion View. Assistant Organizers can do everything else.

Email Group Members

To locate the *Email Members* form, scroll over the *Group Tools* link on the right of your Meetup group home page toolbar and click *Email Members*.

The *Email Members* form has several options. Choose to send a message to *All Members* on the Mailing List or you can click *See More Options* for several choices.

- A *custom list* allows you to create a modified mailing list.
- *Members on the mailing list* will send the message to all Members who have chosen to be on the Mailing list.
- *Active Members* have logged in in the past 30 days.
- *Inactive Members* have not logged in in the past 30 days.
- *Organizers* are Members who have been assigned a Leadership Team role by you.
- *Related to a specific Meetup event* allows you choose a Meetup event and then offers selections to get more specific about which Members will receive your message.

If you choose *Replies*, go to *Mailing List* to send an email, any replies will go to you and all the members on the mailing list. Note that I don't recommend this option, as it can lead to problems.

Below these settings, you'll find a form. You can either:

- Type your message straight into the box, using the menu to format your content; or
- Paste HTML-formatted code by clicking *HTML* in the top menu bar, and pasting your code.

Check *Also post message on this Meetup Group's Message Board* to add this to your Board.

To preview your work, click *Preview* at the bottom of the page.

When you're all set, click *Submit*.

Meetup Event Emails

Once you've scheduled a Meetup event, you'll have the option to *Send It* as an announcement to your group. You may also delay the announcement until a later time. Either way, make certain that you announce the event at least two weeks prior to the event. If you do not use the *Send It* option, the only way members will know about a new Meetup event is by visiting the home page or calendar. I'd venture to guess that most people wouldn't do this on a regular basis.

You can also set up automatic reminders about Meetup events when you schedule them.

Personal Email via Meetup

It is simple to send a personal email message to another member. Go to their profile page and click on the envelope icon adjacent to their profile picture. A slash mark on the member envelope icon indicates that the member has limited who can contact them through the site.

Meetup allows a maximum of twelve Member-to-Member messages per day. This limitation is designed to prevent spamming.

Contact your members on a regular basis to keep up the momentum of your Meetup group and make sure that everyone is up to date on group activities and announcements.

14 – Marketing and Promoting Your Meetup Group

There are endless ways to increase the membership of your Meetup group through marketing and promotions. In addition to the built-in Meetup marketing tools, social media should be your go-to source. Social media is all the rage, not to mention that it's free. I'm happy to share a list of marketing resources that I use, but there are hundreds, if not thousands. So, spend some time doing research to see what else you can find. Always think creatively!

Link Exchange

Exchanging links with other Meetup organizers can be very helpful, especially when it comes to search engine optimization. The best way to do this is to contact other Meetup Organizers that you know and ask them if they would be willing to do a link exchange. This is basically a professional courtesy among Meetup organizers and is also a great way to support and promote each other as unpaid sponsors.

Share Meetup Events With Social Media

Facebook, Twitter, LinkedIn, Pinterest, Foursquare, Instagram, YouTube, and *Google Places/Local*

Create a Facebook Fan Page for your Meetup Group and post events, notices, invitations, relevant information, and articles. The Fan Page will mirror your Meetup site and help you reach a wider audience.

Add content on your social media sites at least once or twice daily. There are many places and websites available to find great content. The first place to start is Google. This is where you will create Google alerts for keywords and topics that would be of interest to potential members.

Ask Members to Check-in At Your Meetup Events
It's easy to let others know you've arrived at a Meetup event. Checking in to a Meetup event makes it easy for members to see who's there and find the group.

You can check-in and view other members who have checked-in on the Meetup Android app, the Meetup iPhone application, or using one of the third-party Meetup apps that support check-ins.

Members who check-in to events are also noted as in attendance for the event so you're also helping the organizer track attendance.

15 – Sponsors For Your Meetup Group

When to Start Looking For a Sponsor(s)
Have a few meetings under your belt and an established track record before approaching potential sponsors. You will also want a reasonable amount of dedicated members. Sponsors want to know that others are seeing their investment. "You need customers to get customers" is kind of like the chicken and egg argument, but it's true. You'll know when the time is right to approach sponsorships, and sometimes the sponsors will approach you.

Why Do You Need a Sponsor
You may not need a sponsor if you charge membership dues or an entrance fee to attend your Meetups. If you're not charging anything, then the money for your Meetup subscription, name tags, printing, paper, advertising and other miscellaneous supplies or services will have to come from somewhere. This is one reason you might want a sponsor. Another one might be for t-shirts, bumper stickers, business cards or printed material to hand out at meetings.

How to Find Sponsors For Your Meetup
Local sponsors are businesses, brands, or other organizations in your community with whom your Meetup group could start a mutually beneficial relationship. A sponsor can provide all sorts of benefits to your Meetup group. Ask questions and find out which potential sponsors would be a good fit for your group.

What Can Your Group Offer A Potential Sponsor
Your members need to be an audience that the sponsor would like as their customers.

What is the topic of your Meetup group and would your members shop at the sponsor's store or use their products?

It's a great idea to provide an overall view of your membership and/or demographics. Most sponsors are looking for brand recognition, advertising, and increased revenue.

Focus on what you have to offer based on the products and services that your members would probably use for their business or personal use.

Offer to list their business on your Meetup site, including their logo, link to their website and contact information, as well as any specials they might offer your members.

Offer to add their information to your monthly flyer or email newsletter.

Offer to display products, handouts, and/or coupons at your check-in table during Meetup events.

Questions To Ask Prospective Sponsor

Have a clear understanding of your sponsor prior to meeting. Know exactly what you're going to ask for before the conversation begins. Are you going to ask the sponsor for donations, door prizes, printed materials, venue, gift cards, etc.? Know exactly what you need and want the sponsor to provide in order to avoid looking unprofessional.

Have various sponsorship levels for potential sponsors that you approach. Delineate sponsorship levels on a document and save it as a PDF to have handy for sponsors and/or advertisers on your Meetup site, newsletter, or social media site. Keep the price list handy to send to potential sponsors via email.

Create a flyer to mail or deliver to potential businesses. Include the following:

- A summary of your Meetup group
- Describe a typical Meetup
- Be specific about what you need or expect from them
- How they can benefit from sponsoring your group? Remember that everyone is walking around with that invisible sign on their forehead that reads, "What's in it for me?" Be ready to answer that question.

How to Add A Sponsor To Your Meetup Site

Once you've found a sponsor and reached an agreement, add their image, information, and a link to their website to the *Sponsors and Perks* section of your group. It is simple to do. Click on *Sponsors* in your group navigation bar and then click *Add a Sponsor.*

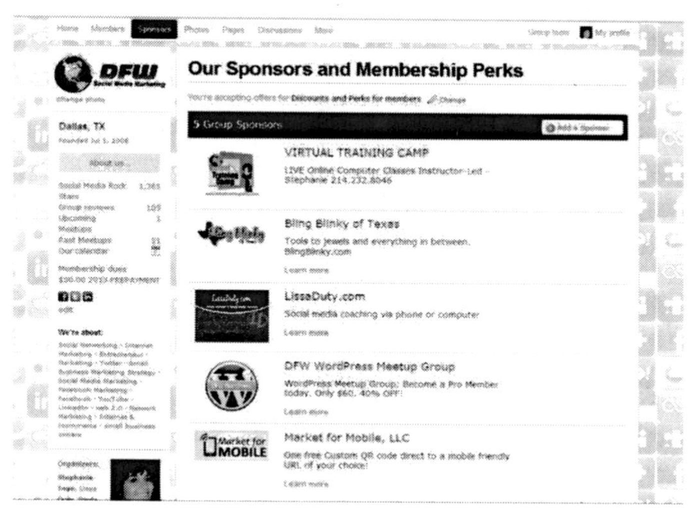

Enter the sponsor's name, a description of what they're providing, and a link to their website. You can also upload their logo or an image to represent them by clicking *Add a Photo.* Click *Submit.*

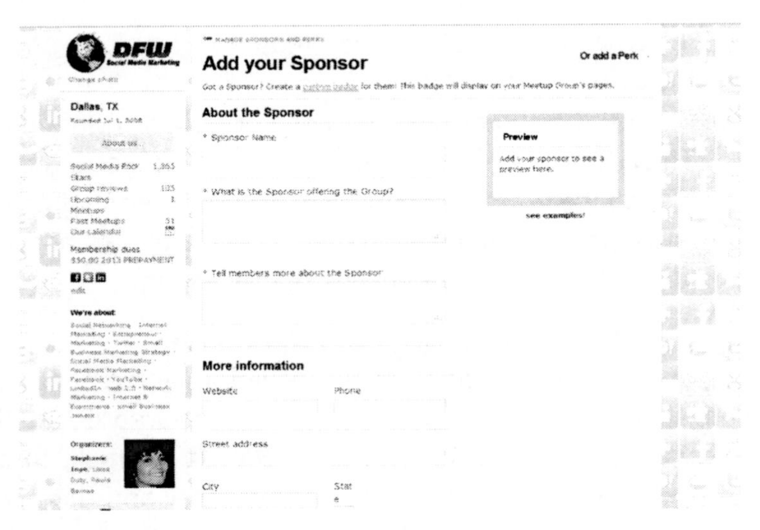

Don't forget to send an email to your members, announcing the new sponsor. List any perks that they are offering to your members.

Local businesses are always looking for ways to get the word out about their products and/or services, and there are several eBay Certified Solution Providers who are willing to sponsor local Meetup groups. It's always a great idea to place flyers, coupons, or business cards at your check-in table to help get the word out about your sponsors.

Always mention sponsors in your *Group description* on other *Pages*, or on your Meetup group *Message Boards.* Offer to talk about them in the messages you send your Meetup members and/or offer to acknowledge their support during your Meetup event.

Note: You're a local community leader, and your Meetup group has a lot to offer potential sponsors! It's much easier than you might think to get sponsors, so don't be afraid or intimidated when it comes to asking.

16 – Seeing Other Meetups at Work

In the next few chapters, I want you to hear from some key Meetups that have started with only one or two people and grown exponentially. They have taught me about the power of people and the desire to connect with others who share their dreams and passion. Both are powerful forces and can unite complete strangers.

The desire to connect to like-minded individuals is the common denominator for most Meetup organizers, including myself. Technology, ecommerce and marketing are very popular topics and attract large numbers; however, groups with largest number of members are the ones focusing on hiking, nature and adventure.

As you can see, there is wide range of topics, so no matter what your interest is, you can probably find a group to join by doing a quick search on the Meetup site.

If you happen to be searching for an eBay group, the good news is that there are approximately fifty groups throughout the world with new groups forming all the time; there are 711 business-related groups, but fitness leads the way with 6,330 groups at the time of this writing and with the largest number of members.

With the growing popularity of being an entrepreneur and the high unemployment rate, many people are now working from home or the nearest coffee shop. Being your own boss has many perks, but one of thing that's missing is 'shop talk'. Stay-at-home-moms (SAHM) typically love their job, but they still have that need for adult conversation. Thank goodness for Meetup!

Since 2005 when I was first introduced to Meetup, I have had the pleasure getting to know many other group organizers in person and online. It's always fun to put a face with a name and that's exactly what Meetup does, putting the social back into social media.

I am honored and delighted to introduce you to some of my fellow Meetup organizers who were willing to share their stories, tips and tricks, and best recommendations in hopes of helping you achieve success in your Meetup group. Meet Chris Taylor of San Francisco, Rich Siok of Chicago, Michelle Gauvreau in Connecticut, Bruce Zalkin in Sarasota, Florida, Bobbi Miller and Robbin Levin in New Hampshire, and Danni Ackerman in Las Vegas. These folks have grown their Meetup groups from a handful to several hundred with Chris Taylor leading the way.

17 - Bay Area eBay & eCommerce Sellers

Leader/Oganizer: Chris Taylor
Co-Organizers: Alan Gilson, Sherry Gilson, Nancy Nelson, and Serena Lee
URL: http://www.meetup.com/eBay-Sellers

Almost 750 sellers from beginning-never-even-listed all the way through eBay trained Education Specialists, our members come from all over the San Francisco Bay Area. They are a great group of sellers who love to help others succeed by sharing their expertise and experiences.

We typically meet the last Tuesday or Wednesday of each month.

Usually we meet in the south Bay Area, but try to move our meetings around to make it easier for more members to attend. We cover a pretty wide geography.

Four years ago, I joined Page Mage. We provide applications for ecommerce sellers – from branding to cross-selling and soon social media marketing. It was important for us to understand the people we wanted to use our products. Originally that meant joining an eBay seller Meetup group in the Bay Area and hearing directly the needs and frustrations of sellers as well as the successes. But surprisingly one did not exist, so we started our own.

The first Meetup for our group had five people. The second one had six people, three of whom were the same (including myself). I strongly considered giving up. But there were two members who'd come to each meeting and were extremely knowledgeable. They were also wonderful women who were happy to help others. So they convinced me we should keep the group going. Our third Meetup featured a guest speaker. She'd run interactive marketing for the Coca Cola Company. Suddenly, we had 19 people attend! It was pretty exciting!!

Since then we've tried to make sure each month we have a topic of value to the members. We meet regularly, even through the summer. I try and map out topics many months in advance that connect to the time of year as well as to topics that are particularly hot in the minds of sellers. We try and consistently meet the last week of each month. And listen.

Always listen to the members to make sure that the group is providing value to them.

Perhaps the biggest challenge is finding venues. We are fortunate to meet every few months at eBay but also use area restaurants and some free office meeting space. With restaurants, always check out the space at the time your meetup would be held.

We've had some nightmares where it was so loud it was too difficult to hear the presenters. It's nice to have food options for attendees at restaurants but then it's more difficult to have formal presentations. So we mix things up.

My Best Meetup Tips:
Keep at it. Don't get discouraged. The more you meet, the more others will find out about it and the more your group will grow.

Find at least one Co-Organizer, as quickly as possible, somebody you can bounce ideas off of and ideally, to help pull together each Meetup.

Try different things. New venues, try formal presentations and panel discussions. See what works.

Periodically ask your members what would be valuable to them.

Connect on *Facebook* and elsewhere with other group leaders so we all help each other.

— Chris Taylor

18 - The Chicagoland Area eBay Seller Meetup Group

Leader/Organizer: Rich Siok
Co-Organizers: Nila Siok, Bev England
URL: http://www.meetup.com/entrepreneur-940

My wife, Nila, and I met the folks from Meetup.com while attending the eBay Live Convention in Las Vegas in 2006. We talked with the owners, and he mentioned starting a sellers' group in Chicago. After seeing all the eBay Sellers in Vegas, we thought this would be a great way to meet other sellers and potentially meet people interested in taking a Basics of Selling class. Nila and I are both Education Specialists.

We returned home to Chicago and gave it a try. We began meeting at a Panera Bread Coffee/Sandwich Shop. For the first several months, we had only a couple folks show up. One month, we had no one show, and we just sat with each other and had dinner. Then, I decided to post the meeting on the free board at Panera, and we began to grow a little more each month.

It wasn't until Jim "Griff" Griffith came to visit our group in 2009 that we really grew. He announced the meeting on his show, and we had about 45 attend his meeting. The rest is history. We now have 630 members and are overwhelmed with all the great folks we meet.

Recommendations For New Meetup Organizers
It's best to have your meetings in public places. Some people are very leery of meeting new people.

Choose a time that is convenient.

Be consistent with the time and date. I have mine the second Wednesday of each month at 6:15 p.m. unless we have a special guest.

Since we are the organizers, the meetings are held at a location convenient for us. If folks want you to hold it elsewhere, suggest they open their own group. I know that sounds a little rough, but I got to tell you from experience that members will give you a million opinions on what to do and how to do this and that. I know what works best for us, and that's what makes us successful.

Never have a meeting including food and expect to collect the money at the meeting. You will never collect enough to pay the bill.

Trying to find a location that accepts individual checks for dinners can be difficult, but have a talk with the owner and explain what you want to do. This can be hard but keep looking. The location we have now was going to charge for the room if we didn't order a certain amount of food, but we have exceeded that each month. They are happy and we are too. They have WiFi and a free screen.

Be professional. You are a networking group and want to share ideas and things that make you successful eBay sellers.

Lose the negative people that want to take over meetings – remove them from your membership.

Get guest speakers to help you out. Many from your group may be able to help like photos, thrifting, etc.

Have fun!

Enlist the help of co-organizers to help with your group. I have two, my wife Nila and Bev England. They can help by giving different perspectives and help when hosting events.

Find sponsors to help fund your group. Expenses arise for the group. Examples are Meetup fees, costs for the venue renting, audio visual, printing material and ink, purchasing a projector and screen, etc. We also cover the cost of guest speakers' dinners and limo or taxi service for them from the hotel airport and back, etc. We also cover the costs of the organizer's and co-organizers' dinners in our fees; it's a small perk for all the time spent organizing the monthly events.

Charge a fee for your events to help defer the above costs. Tell your members that it's an investment in their business. This helps keep all the free loaders that really don't sell on eBay or are just looking to bother other serious sellers for FREE help. I know this sounds a little rough, but you will run across a few of these folks.

Ask Griff to announce the meetings on eBay Radio every week.

Invite Griff to come visit your group as soon as you can.

Join your local Chamber of Commerce and attend their networking events. Spread the word on their website and in newsletters.

Use Facebook, Twitter, Pinterest, and email to get the word out.

— Rich Siok

19 - Connecticut eBay & Commerce Sellers

Leader/Organizer: Michelle Gauvreau
AssistantOrganizers: Catherine DeVald, Dory
URL: http://www.meetup.com/CT-eBay-and-eCommerce-Sellers-Group

How the Connecticut Meetup Group got started ...

My name is Michelle Rice Gauvreau, Organizer of the Connecticut eBay and ecommerce Sellers Meetup Group.

After attending an eBay Radio Conference in 2010, I decided to start my own eBay sellers group, never realizing how far it would come to be what it is today – a very popular group with 121 members and growing. I am very proud of this fabulous group.

The reason I started the group was simply to gain motivation in sales and to help other sellers gain the same knowledge as well as to help enhance their online businesses with simple tools from online selling venues.

I had much support from my online selling peers all over the country and have received a lot of great ideas since 2010; I have cultivated and grown a family with my members, and that is key in building any group. Without them, our group would not exist. Now that the group is in its own realm, I leave it this year, knowing that it will go even further than I dreamed and that is the best feeling.

I have been blessed to get to know so many people in the industry – many big names to add to the board, from the well-known speakers to the experienced and new sellers.

Starting your own group takes time, thought and patience. Patience is virtue in all scenarios. Sometimes you'll have easy Meetup events and other times, yes, I admit it, you'll be tearing your hair out or you'll be very nervous especially when having a speaker. Trust me, I've been there! Don't be afraid to ask for help from your members – they are very willing to help. You get through each and every Meetup event with more insight than you ever had before. You gain the knowledge and respect as the organizer of your group.

Learn as you grow and over time, you'll gain sponsors, as well. Sponsors help to spread the word about your group. Networking and social media are key components, as well. I encourage anyone who does not have an eBay seller Meetup Group in their area to start one. If you're unsure, please reach out to any eBay organizer, as we're here for you and willing to lend our support.

I've learned so much over the last three years (and even before that going to the conferences since 2007), met so many sellers from all walks of life, and made so many friends from all over the world. It's an amazing journey and one that I hope to continue, as I step down from my leadership role and continue on a new path in the world of ecommerce.

Happy Selling to you all!

— Michelle Gauvreau

20 - The Sarasota eBay Sellers Meetup Group

Leader/Organizer: Bruce Zalkin
AssistantOrganizer: Jon Wagner
URL: http://www.meetup.com/The-Sarasota-Ebay-Sellers-meet-up-Group

Best practices for anyone wanting to start or lead an eBay group: Listen to your membership, some people will know more about eBay than you. I seem to learn something new at every meeting.

Have the group focus on eBay and selling/buying. For us, this is a learning group, not a networking group. I had to ask someone to stop promoting their web design company at our meetings. They were just trying to drum up business.

If you build it, they will come. In the beginning we only had 2, or 3 people attend our meetings, now, we have 25+ every month and a waiting list. Do not get discouraged and make sure the meetings are the same time and place every month.

— Bruce Zalkin

21 - Seacoast eBay Sellers

Leader/Organizer: Bobbi Miller
URL: meetup.com/Seacoast-Ebay-Seller-Group

Why did you start the Meetup group?
I enjoy networking with other ecommerce sellers. I wanted to build our seller community here in New England. I've started other groups in the past, and I knew I had the skills to grow a Sellers Group.

When did you start the group?
Our group began in the Spring 2009.

What were some of the obstacles that you faced as a group leader/organizer?
Finding a free place to meet that had adequate parking and was centrally located.

How to market and promote the group, in order for eBay sellers to find us. We began before eBay was really promoting seller groups.

How did you decide on a name for your group?
I knew we needed to have the word eBay in the title so folks could find us on Meetup.com, but I wanted to have ecommerce in the title so folks knew we would talk about other platforms.

Tell us about your first meeting? How many attended? Where did you meet? What did you talk about? Did you have an agenda?
We began at the local library and three people showed up. We talked about what topics we would like to talk about in the future.

Does your group focus on eBay only, or do you also discuss other platforms, such as Amazon, Etsy, etc.?
We have discussed eBay, Amazon and apps or products that are used to help sellers such as Outright, Terapeak, etc.

How did you select a venue? What criteria do you look for when selecting a venue?
Criteria: Food (individual meal tickets), easy parking, centrally located (we serve 3 States in New England) and private room.

Do you have regular meetings? If so, are they always on the same day of the week? What made you choose that particular day?
We began by meeting monthly, but went to every other month. I polled the members on Meetup and we found Monday and Tuesday nights are best for our meetings.

Tell us about your most memorable moment as organizer? Your favorite meeting? Your favorite guest speaker?
I enjoy seeing how happy our members are to network with each other. Our members have formed friendships from attending the group. My favorite meetings are probably our Christmas Holiday Yankee Swap because we just have a lot of fun and exchange gifts. Favorite speakers have been Griff (3 times now) and Chris Green. Oh, and Jason Smith!

If we were a fly on the wall, what would we see at a typical meeting?
We stay on a schedule because we have some folks traveling an hour or more. We meet at 6:00 p.m. We order food 6:30

p.m., Speaker 7:00 - 8:30 p.m. We always begin with a free raffle on an eBayana item and have announcements and intro the speaker.

Do you have a check-in table? Do you hand out name tags? Who works the check-in table?
I print up name tags. I have a volunteer at the check-in table where we have literature from our sponsors and free items if they have been given.

Do you have assistant organizers? How did you select them?
Robbin has recently taken over the group. I never had an assistant organizer, but I did ask for folks to help with different things.

Do you have sponsors? If so, how did you find them and approach them about becoming a sponsor?
I approached the sponsors. We have had Stamps.com, Terapeak, and Bubblefast. It is easier than you would think. Most say yes.

How much do you charge sponsors?
$75 per year and we promote them and put their literature out at every Meetup event.

Do you have membership dues? If so, how much do you charge?
We don't have dues, but we are now charging $3-5 via PayPal to RSVP. We never did this before, but this now seems to decrease the no-shows, which have always been frustrating.

Do you charge an entrance fee for monthly meetings? If so, how much do you charge?
See answer above.

What is your best advice for someone who is on the fence about starting their own eBay Meetup group?
Start small, have fun, and ask for help from the others that have gone before.

What is the one thing you would advise against for organizers?
Keep things positive. Don't allow a few to ruin the group for the whole. We've banned members for various reasons. Make sure folks know this is not a class, but a group for seasoned sellers. I ask that folks sell for at least six months, prior to joining.

Have you ever had a member who was a trouble maker? If so, how did you handle the situation?
Yes, we have had folks come to promote their own business, and I will go talk with them and make it clear that is not the purpose of the group. They usually don't come back.

Do you have a Facebook group for your Meetup group? If so, do you have help maintaining it?

Yes, we have a Facebook group, but I ask that folks first become a member of the Meetup group before joining the Facebook group.

How do you market your meetings?
I use our Facebook group, Twitter and eBay Radio.

— Bobbi Miller

22 - The Dallas eBaybes & eMales

Leader/Oganizer: Stephanie Inge
Assistant Organizers: Terry Thayer, Dan Goins, Martha Oberman, Herb Oberman, Peyton Weaver and Jim Halloran
URL: http://www.meetup.com/dallasebaybesandemales/

It was 2001, and I still remember reading that interesting article about an eBay seller in Atlanta, named Angie, who hosted a meeting of eBay sellers at a local restaurant. As an eBay seller of two years, I knew first-hand just how isolating this job could be, spending several hours a day in front of a computer screen or behind a camera taking photos.

Networking, social media and camaraderie were non-existent in my life at that time, and I longed to meet others who could relate to my daily routine. Needless to say the article piqued my interest, and after reading it, I was determined to learn more. I located Angie and fired off an email, asking her a million questions. She was very nice, helpful and encouraged me to start a Dallas eBay Group.

That I did! I was hell-bent and determined to do this after reading the article and her email reply. The decision was made and I set out to create the greatest group that ever existed.

Living in Texas where everything is big, we feel the need to do everything in grand style and larger than life. After doing some preliminary research, I managed to find a small group of eBay sellers who were planning to meet in November 2001. I emailed Lou Fausak and brazenly asked him if I could join them. Luckily he said, "Yes," and in retrospect, it was a life-changing decision.

That meeting was near Fort Worth, Texas, and quite a drive from my home, but I was motivated and had a clear vision. I needed to experience a meeting of eBay sellers, so I could get a feel for what they talk about and how to be a good leader. To be quite honest, it wasn't a meeting, but a group of very nice folks having dinner, cocktails and talking about eBay. Since eBay was one of my favorite topics, I thoroughly enjoyed myself and made some new friends.

Back in those early days of eBay, trips to the local post office were a part of my daily routine and a social outing for me, as I would occasionally spot a fellow eBay seller, and thirty minutes later, we were best buddies. I could always spot and connect with another eBay seller, as we're a different breed.

The questions are always the same, even to this day.

I wonder what their eBay ID is?

I wonder what their feedback rating is?

I wonder how long they've been selling?

I wonder how successful they are?

I wonder where they find stuff to sell?

These are all common questions for eBay sellers; however, there is one question that you would never ask another seller and that is, "Where do you find your stuff to sell?" That is a huge no-no and as they say, "If I told you, I'd have to kill you!"

From the very beginning, I was hooked on eBay and enjoyed singing the praises of how great it was to be an eBay seller. Basically, I was an eBay cheerleader and not much has changed since those early days, in spite of all the changes we've experienced in the past fourteen years.

I consider myself an unofficial eBay ambassador and enjoy teaching others how to start and succeed in their own eBay business. eBay is still the single best ecommerce site for ecommerce merchants to get their start and do so on a shoestring budget.

Fast forward to January 4, 2002, a group of approximately fifteen eBay sellers met at the original Chili's located on Greenville Avenue in Dallas. At that time, there was no such thing as social media and the only tools available to get the word out about the new group were email, newsgroups, Yahoo Groups, Craigslist, eBay discussion forums and Evite.

For the first three years, these were the methods of communication used to market and grow the membership. With each passing month, the numbers continued to increase, which brought new challenges. Eventually, we moved to a larger restaurant that had a private room, were willing to do separate checks, was moderately priced and had plenty of parking.

In the beginning meetings were informal and basically a gathering of eBay sellers to talk about all things eBay. Occasionally one of the members would speak or do a presentation on shipping, customer service, etc.; however, there was no specific agenda until the third or fourth year. By that time, we had a couple hundred members, and it was easy to get guest speakers since we could offer a captive audience of eBay and online sellers.

Attending the annual eBay conference, eBay Live, was a fantastic way to meet vendors, speakers and eBay staff. It provided the perfect opportunity to introduce myself, tell them about Dallas eBaybes & eMales and ask if they'd be interested in coming to Dallas to speak – much more effective than a cold call or a random email.

Ever since the first meeting, nearly twelve years ago, we have met on the fourth Monday of each month, except November and December, since the meeting date falls too close to Thanksgiving and Christmas. In early December we have an informal holiday get-together, usually with a White Elephant Gift Exchange. Come January, it starts all over again. Wash, rinse, repeat!

Many of our original members are still active and attend regular meetings and, over the years, have become extended family. In the early years, meetings were very informal and consisted of dinner and lots of eBay talk. Meetings have evolved and we now have an agenda that consists of a free one-hour class, dinner and a guest speaker, power-seller panel or round table discussion.

For the past five years or more, I've had assistant organizers who are a tremendous help to me with meeting plans, working the front door, coordinating door prizes and more. It is very nice to share the responsibilities and know that you have people that you can rely on.

Two things that have always set eBay apart from every other ecommerce platform were the online auction format and the strong sense of community. To this day, both of them are very important to me as an eBay merchant and as a local community leader of the Dallas eBaybes & eMales Meetup Group. Long before the advent of social media, there were eBay discussion boards and eBay community groups, which were alive with friendly chatter and where I've met many eBay friends.

I'd be remiss if I didn't mention the days of eBay Live, 2002-2007, with the last one held in Chicago 2007. Some of the other host cities included New Orleans, San Jose, Las Vegas and Boston, and it was the highlight of the year for thousands of eBay sellers. A few years later came eBay on Location, a very intimate one-day conference, limited to 500 attendees. The last EOL was held in 2012.

In 2013, eBay decided to host local events, partnering with the various eBay-seller Meetup Groups. The Bay Area eBay & ecommerce Sellers was first and was held in San Jose in August 2012. One week later, The Dallas eBaybes & eMales in Dallas, Texas, and Chicagoland Area eBay & Ecommerce Sellers, September 11th in Chicago, Illinois.

Let's talk about guest speakers, which is somewhat of a numbers game and present certain challenges. Large groups provide captive audiences and make it easier to attract quality guest speakers. Without great speakers, it's difficult to get large audiences. Enlist the help of veteran eBay sellers and/or Education Specialists, who may be willing to volunteer and teach classes before or during your meetings.

Classes were originally designed to help newbie sellers, and guest speakers were geared for the seasoned veterans. As Organizer, I try to please everyone, which can be quite challenging. Create a poll and ask members for their suggestions and ideas for meeting topics and possible classes.

The first big break for Dallas eBaybes came in August 2006, following the eBay live event in Las Vegas. Meg Whitman flew nine eBay staffers to Dallas to speak at our August meeting. One of the staffers was her personal bodyguard, as eBay has always been very big on security. We had a huge turnout as one would expect and the meeting was a tremendous success.

Since that time, we've experienced many milestones, including a private Ice Cream Social hosted by John Donahoe, President and CEO of eBay, Inc., in May 2010. We enlisted him as an honorary member and presented him with an official Dallas eBaybes & eMales shirt.

One of our most popular eBay guests is, Jim "Griff" Griffith, author of the *Official eBay Bible* and Dean of eBay Education. Griff usually visits us every year, and it's always a very special occasion that everyone looks forward to. eBay, Inc sent several VIP's to Dallas for our 10th Anniversary celebration in 2012, which was super special.

Being the Organizer and leader of your own eBay seller group can open many doors and be extremely gratifying. The most important recommendation for anyone who is considering starting their own Meetup Group is to do it with passion and for the right reasons.

Most of the rewards are intangible and invaluable and as they say, "There are some things that you can't buy with MasterCard." Do it for the right reasons and you'll never regret it.

Regular monthly meetings are extremely beneficial and educational. Regardless of your level of eBay experience, you'll learn something at every meeting, in addition to networking with fellow eBay sellers.

For many years we had two meetings per month, a monthly luncheon for members who are unable to attend the regular meetings and regular meetings on the fourth Monday of the month from 6:00pm to 8:30pm.

Luncheons were planned, scheduled and coordinated by one of our assistant organizers, so it was very enjoyable and no extra work for me. My goal for 2014 is to resume monthly luncheons for those who aren't able to attend the regularly scheduled meetings.

With each passing year, eBay evolves and becomes more mainstream, which requires sellers to adapt and evolve also. The marketplace has become much more competitive, so savvy eBay sellers must protect their product sources with every fiber of their being.

eBay Selling Tip: If you can find a wholesale product source on the Internet by Googling it, so can a million/billion other people. Be resourceful and think outside the box.

Membership in a local eBay group will make you a much more savvy and connected eBay seller and provide a support channel that is unlike any other. If your city/town doesn't have an eBay seller group, I highly recommend that you start one and I am here to mentor you each and every step of the way.

In summary, The Dallas eBaybes & eMales, my very first Meetup Group, has evolved into an extended family over the past twelve years and has been a labor of love. When I think of the future of my eBay Meetup Group, I am reminded of the "I Have a Dream" speech by Dr. Martin Luther King, Jr. (one of my all-time favorites). I too have a dream, although mine is much different and not nearly as profound.

My dream has always been to write a book and to have a chapter of eBaybes & eMales in all 50 states before I get my final boarding pass for the big bus in the sky. My pledge to anyone wanting to start their very own chapter is and always has been, to mentor anyone and everyone each and every step of the way to help them achieve their Meetup goals.

23 - Las Vegas eBay Amazon eCommerce Online Sellers Group

Organizer: Danni Ackerman
Co-Organizer: Dawn Ralston
Assistant Organizer: Martha David
URL: http://www.meetup.com/LasVegasOnlineSellers/

You'd think Las Vegas would be an incredibly easy place to form a Meetup Group. It's really like any other big city in that respect; regular people leading regular lives and finding those that want to build and grow an online business has the same difficulties as other places.

I started my first Meetup Group up in Reno, Nevada. It really is as easy as setting up the Meetup over at the Meetup.com website. Use a good description and keywords to describe your group so it can be found by the right people. That's my first bit of advice. Tagging your group with keywords, such as eBay and ecommerce will bring your group in front of other online sellers.

Don't worry about starting small. My first organized Meetup event was in Reno, Nevada, and attended by a handful of people. We met at a local restaurant, enjoyed good conversation and networking right from the start. The really great thing about Meetup events is how diverse the knowledge base is of the people who attend.

When I moved down to Las Vegas, I was surprised to find there was no active eBay seller group. I used the experience gained from my Reno group and put it into action. As an

Organizer, you are allowed to have three groups under your account. There is a $72.00 charge every six months for group organizers. Getting sponsors really helps with this; companies who sell products or services related to ecommerce are usually willing to step up and help.

The Las Vegas Online Sellers Meetup Group started with about thirty members attending the first meeting, due to having a celebrity as special guest, well an eBay celebrity anyway. Jim "Griff" Griffith kicked us off right, and it was a great start to the group. We met at a local casino event room, which was surprisingly affordable. I was able to get Kabbage.com to sponsor the room, and it set a professional tone for the meetings to come.

We have since moved into a local restaurant with a separate room that houses our 40-50 monthly attendees quite nicely. As an Organizer, I arrange a different person to speak on a topic each month.

We vary the subjects to cover all aspects of online selling. It's real people sharing real experience and the interaction with the crowd makes for fantastic learning for all!

Tips I would give to future Meetup Group Organizers:

- Book your meeting at least two weeks in advance to give people time to RSVP.
- Have a sign-in sheet and know who are your regular attendees.
- Have some goodies to give away as door prizes.
- Use a raffle to raise funds for the Meetup. We were able to raise money for a projector and screen.
- Take good care of your speaker guests! Pay for their dinner and provide transportation if needed.
- Have Co-Organizers and Assistant Organizers you can count on.

It's really not hard to put together a quality Meetup Group, but it can be some work maintaining one. The Las Vegas Group is now more than 225 members strong and growing all the time! It's a great way to meet the people in your community who love doing the same thing you are, selling online.

—Danni Ackerman, www.TheDanniApp.com

24 - New England eBay & eCommerce Sellers Group

Organizer: Robbin Levin

URL: http://www.meetup.com/Seacoast-Ebay-Seller-Group/

My Meetup Group was started by Bobbi Miller and was founded April 9, 2009. I recently took over as group organizer because Bobbi asked me if I would be interested in the role, as she is moving to Florida next year. Luckily, she'll be here to guide and mentor me along the way until leaving for Florida next year and will continue to be an active member of our Meetup community. For me, adjusting to my new role as Meetup Organizer and filling the shoes of Bobbi Miller will be a challenge, as she has done such a fantastic job ever since I can remember.

When I showed up for my very first meeting, I was not sure what to expect. I was such a novice eBay and ecommerce merchant. I was immediately embraced by my fellow colleagues and instantly caught a fever to grow my knowledge and business. It was March 9, 2011, and the topic was: How to Organize your Time, Space, Inventory to Build a More Profitable Business

What a wonderful introduction to Meetup events and my fellow like-minded associates. I was instantly hooked and knew I would be attending every meeting from then on. I think I have only missed two meetings since that day.

Our group is really special. Although we focus on eBay, we encompass all ecommerce business. We try to stay current and cutting edge. Again, Bobbi Miller has done a spectacular job. Big shoes to fill, but I will rise to and meet this challenge.

We recently relocated our Meetup events to The Roundabout Diner in Portsmouth, New Hampshire, located at the Portsmouth Traffic Circle. This is a great location and centrally located for our members to attend. They also have a full menu and bar at our fingertips with a private function room and podium and screen for presenters. It has a great function room with enough seating to hold all of our members if needed.

We try to have regular meetings on average about every six weeks. We often have our meetings on Tuesdays, but have been known to switch that up according to the availability of our speakers.

Being new to the role as Organizer, I must say one of my most memorable moments was when Bobbi asked me to take over the job. I was so honored and excited to have been chosen to keep the group going. We have had so many terrific meetings & topics presented. It would be hard to choose a favorite Meetup event, as Bobbi has always kept things current and interesting.

In the past, we have handed out name tags at the check-in table so we all know each other's name.

If I were a fly on the wall, I would have to say that the topics and enthusiasm of this group is infectious.

We currently have no assistant organizers, but always willing and helpful participation when needed. We are never in short supply of helpers.

We have several sponsors, which Bobbi has selected and set up: Terapeak, Bubblefast, and Stamps.com. I have only added one new sponsor since taking over on July 19, 2013, Danna Crawford, Power Selling Mom & Virtual Online Learning. She has been an amazing support and mentor, so this was a no-brainer for me. I am currently looking to add sponsors to our group.

We don't charge membership dues, but do charge a Meetup fee of $5.00 to attend each meeting, which helps to offset miscellaneous fees.

If you are considering starting a Meetup Group in your area, I suggest just doing it. It will be gratifying and help connect with local like-minded entrepreneurs. It doesn't take much more than a little effort and organizing to get going. Be careful to keep current with information. Make sure you do not let meetings get off track, but suggest having open discussions for questions towards the end of the meeting. If a member needs to stay afterwards, offer to do that to answer any off-topic questions.

If a member becomes a problem, such as body odor or being rude, simply have a private talk with them to address any issues. Should the problem continue, the best solution is to remove them. Remember, you're the leader, so make sure that you're doing what is in the best interest of the entire group.

We have a group *Facebook* fan page -

https://www.facebook.com/groups/NewEnglandebayMeetup/

At this time, I maintain the fan page by myself and use it to market our events with a little help from my friends and through our Meetup page.

I market our meetings on this page, as well as word of mouth, sponsorship help (from Danna Crawford), social media, and the Meetup site.

Meetup Organizer 4-Week Quick-Start Guide

Four Weeks Prior to Your First Meeting

- ❑ Find venue and make arrangements with venue management.
- ❑ Decide on a topic.
- ❑ Decide what type of Meetup (class, panel discussion, guest speaker, networking, or round table group discussion, etc.).
- ❑ If you're going to have a speaker, ask them to email you a bio, headshot/logo, presentation outline/bullet list.
- ❑ Schedule Meetup event on group calendar and include event description and agenda.
- ❑ Announce the Meetup event via email and social media.
- ❑ Create an event on your *Facebook* group fan page.
- ❑ Sign up for *Square* account at www.squaredup.com and order the free credit card reader for your smartphone.
- ❑ Sign up for *Paypal Here* account at www.paypal.com and order the free credit card reader for your smartphone.

Three Weeks Prior to

- ❑ Post announcement once a day on your *Facebook* group fan page and *Twitter* page.
- ❑ Tweak the event description, if necessary. Make sure to include any and all details:
    - Venue with address and link to a Google map
    - Time
    - Guest Speaker

- Topic
- Agenda
- Will food and beverage be served?
- Cost (if any)
- Door Prizes (if any)

Two Weeks Prior

- ❑ Continue posting announcements on *Facebook* and *Twitter* at least once a day.
- ❑ Post the event on *Craigslist* in the Meetings Category.
- ❑ Send email reminder to members who have not RSVP'd.
- ❑ Send email to guest speaker to confirm and if you haven't received the information from them, remind them to do so ASAP.
- ❑ Ask members if they'd be willing to donate door prizes.

One Week Prior to

- ❑ Call or send email to confirm your event with venue management and provide current headcount.
- ❑ Send email reminder to members who have not RSVP'd to the event.
- ❑ Renew/update Craigslist ad so it will appear toward the top of announcements.
- ❑ Post announcements twice each day on Facebook and Twitter.
- ❑ Email your Leadership Team to confirm that they will attend and to share any last minute details that they need to be aware of.
- ❑ Review responses posted on the Meetup event page to see if any require a response.

Two Days Prior to

- ❑ Post announcements 2-3 times daily on *Facebook* and Twitter.
- ❑ Update venue with current headcount.

Day of

- ❑ Make certain that camera is charged and the SD card is in place.
- ❑ Print name tags.
- ❑ Print RSVP list.
- ❑ Print table signs from Meetup site (optional).
- ❑ Create a sign-in sheet so you'll have a record of everyone who attends with contact information. (This is not something that is provided by Meetup.com).
- ❑ Print speaker bio, so you'll be able to give them a proper introduction.
- ❑ Leave early enough to set things up once you arrive at the venue and to be there when guests arrive, so you can greet them.
- ❑ As guests arrive, remind them to check-in with the Meetup mobile app, *Foursquare* and *Facebook*. Create buzz!
- ❑ Once the meeting begins, or when you have time, take lots of pictures and video, if possible.

After Your First Meeting

- ❑ Make sure to say Good-bye to everyone as they're leaving and thank them for coming out!
- ❑ Edit RSVP list on Meetup to mark any No-Shows.
- ❑ Edit event photographs using your favorite image editor.
- ❑ Upload event photos to the Meetup event page and to your *Facebook* group fan page.
- ❑ Post "It was good to see you" for all who attended.
- ❑ Read and review comments to see if any require a response.
- ❑ Send thank you note to guest speaker or panelists.
- ❑ Start planning the next Meetup event, if you haven't done so already!

Resources for the Meetup Organizer

Contact the Author

Stephanie Inge
stephintexas@gmail.com

Search for Existing / Purchase Domain /URL

GoDaddy (http://www.godaddy.com/)

Social Media Marketing / Promotions

Facebook (https://www.facebook.com/)

Pinterest (http://www.pinterest.com/)

Craigslist (http://www.craigslist.org/about/sites#US)

Google+ (https://plus.google.com/)

FourSquare (https://foursquare.com/)

Instagram (http://instagram.com/#)

Google Local (http://www.google.com/+/learnmore/local/)

Twitter (https://twitter.com/)

LinkedIn (http://www.linkedin.com/)

Yelp (http://www.yelp.com/)

Ice Breaker Activities

Resident Assistant (http://www.residentassistant.com/games/)

Mind Tools (http://www.mindtools.com)

Icebreakers (http://www.icebreakers.us/)

Sharon Jaynes
(sharonjaynes.com/wp-content/uploads/2012/01/65-Icebreaker-Ideas-for-Small-Groups.pdf)

Letter Writing Templates
Docstoc (www.docstoc.com/) (sponsorship samples/templates)

SharePDF (http://SharePDF.net)

WikiHow (http://www.wikihow.com/Write-a-Letter-Requesting-Sponsorship)

AZ Templates (http://www.aztemplates.org/) (FREE)

Buzzle (http://www.buzzle.com/)

Sample Words (http://www.samplewords.com/)

Pinterest (pinterest.com/lettersandforms/pins)

Find Relevant Content
Reddit (http://www.reddit.com/)

Stumbleupon (http://www.stumbleupon.com/)

LifeHack (http://www.lifehack.org/)

Storify (http://storify.com/)

Pearltrees (http://www.pearltrees.com/)

GetPrismatic (http://getprismatic.com/)

Themeefy (http://www.themeefy.com/)

Bundlr (http://bundlr.com/)

Scoop.It (http://www.scoop.it/)

Flipboard (https://flipboard.com/)

Meetup Organizer Boot Camp
(http://www.meetup.com/organize/)

Virtual Meetings
Skype (http://www.skype.com/)

Google+ Hangouts on Air
(http://www.google.com/+/learnmore/hangouts/onair.html)

Ustream (http://www.ustream.tv/)

Share Files / Collaborate / Cloud Computing
Drop box (https://www.dropbox.com/)

Google Drive
(http://www.google.com/drive/about.html?authuser=0)

Evernote (https://evernote.com/)

Free Graphics / Stock Images
Grsites (http://www.grsites.com)

Archive (http://www.archive/textures)

Background Labs (http://www.backgroundlabs.com)

Pattern Cooler (http://www.patterncooler.com)

All Free Backgrounds (http://www.allfreebackgrounds.com)

We Graphics (http://www.wegraphics.net/downloads/free-web-backgrounds)

DinPattern (http://www.dinpattern.com)

Squid Fingers (http://www.squidfingers.com/patterns)

Feedio (http://www.background-pictures.feedio.net)

Keyword Tools
Google Keyword Planner
(http://www.googlekeywordplanner.com/)

Wordstream (http://www.wordstream.com/)

Uber Suggest (http://ubersuggest.org/)

KeywordSpy (http://www.keywordspy.com/)

Wordpot (http://www.wordpot.com/)

SEMRush (http://www.semrush.com/)

WordTracker (http://www.wordtracker.com/)

HTML Color Tools for Site Design
Color Scheme Designer
(http://www.colorschemedesigner.com)

Color Combos (http://www.colorcombos.com)

Color Schemer (http://www.colorschemer.com/online.html)

Kuler (https://kuler.adobe.com/create/color-wheel/)

Colors on the Web
(http://www.colorsontheweb.com/colorwheel.asp)

Infohound (http://www.infohound.net/colour)

Check My Colours (http://www.checkmycolours.com)

GPeters (http://www.gpeters.com/color/color-schemes.php)

W3 Schools
(http://www.w3schools.com/tags/ref_colorpicker.asp)

Photo Editing Tools
Picasa (http://picasa.google.com/)

Gimp (http://www.gimp.org/)

PicMonkey (http://www.picmonkey.com/)

Play With Pictures by Vertus
(http://www.vertustech.com/playwithpictures/en/default.php)

Create Interactive Infograms (http://infogr.am/)

HTML Resources
W3 Schools (http://w3schools.com)

HTML Goodies (http://htmlgoodies.com)

HTML Dog (http://htmldog.com)

Page Tutor (http://www.pagetutor.com/index.html)

HTML Net (http://html.net)

Werbach (http://werbach.com/barebones/barebones.html)

Mason (http://mason.gmu.edu/~montecin/htmltags.htm)

HScripts (http://hscripts.com/index.php)

Quackit (http://quackit.com)

Webmonkey (http://webmonkey.com/2010/02/html_cheatsheet)

Added Bytes (http://addedbytes.com)

Simple HTML Guide (http://simplehtmlguide.com)

Net Lingo (http://netlingo.com)

Notes

Notes

Notes

Notes

Notes

Notes

Notes

Notes